David Comyn

The Youthful Exploits of Fionn

David Comyn

**The Youthful Exploits of Fionn**

ISBN/EAN: 9783744736794

Printed in Europe, USA, Canada, Australia, Japan

Cover: Foto ©Suzi / pixelio.de

More available books at **www.hansebooks.com**

*GAELIC UNION PUBLICATIONS.*

# mac-ġníomarṫa Ḟinn.

(Slioċt Saltair Caiṡil.)

## THE YOUTHFUL EXPLOITS

OF

# FIONN.

*The Original Text, from the "Saltair of Cashel," with Modern Irish Version, New Literal Translation, Vocabulary, Notes, and Map.*

EDITED FOR THE GAELIC UNION

BY

## DAVID COMYN,

Editor of *Laoidh Oisin air Thir na n-og; Searc-leanamhain Chriost, &c.*

DUBLIN:
M. H. GILL & SON, 50 UPPER SACKVILLE-ST.
1881.

*This* **Work** *has been named on the Programme of the " Commissioners of Intermediate Education* **in** *Ireland," as a* **text-book** *for Examinations in* **Celtic** *in the Senior* **Grade.** *It has also been placed on the* **Programme** *of Examinations for teachers desirous* **of gaining** *certificates to teach Irish under the Commissioners of National Education.*

PRINTED BY M. H. GILL AND SON, 50 UPPER SACKVILLE-ST., DUBLIN.

# ADVERTISEMENT.

The Gaelic Union at present consists of a number of gentlemen who were some of the founders of the "Society for the Preservation of the Irish Language," and the most active members of the Council of that Society. The immediate object of the Gaelic Union is to publish, at cheap rates, works in the Irish language, original and translated, and to reprint such rare books, or portions of them, as may be required for the use of schools and colleges. The placing of these works within the reach of the people, and in a form useful and accessible to students, is now the great requirement of the movement for the preservation of the Irish language.

By the labours chiefly of the promoters of the Gaelic Union, the Society for the Preservation of the Irish Language has been established, developed, and matured. They have had a very large part in the preparation of the works issued in the name of that society, and in all its other undertakings, and have contributed materially to the success of the movement in obtaining for the Gaelic the position it now holds in schools and colleges of Ireland: they, therefore, understand the requirements of the Gaelic revival movement. Their present undertaking will admit of their efforts being concentrated on the preparation and publication of books, and a periodical for the cultivation of Gaelic. They also make use of the columns of several existing periodicals for this purpose. As they *mean work* they hope to be able to show in connection with the present effort the same energy and perseverance as hitherto, and thereby merit the cordial support and co-operation of every true Gael in and out of Ireland.

Some works there are, the risk of producing which will be borne by publishers. The present is one of this class, and the editors have no concern with any such further than in a literary way. There are many other valuable works, the publication of which would materially improve the present position of Gaelic literature, but which, in the infancy of the movement, it would be risky, if not ruinous, for individuals to undertake. The members of the Gaelic Union, whilst labouring gratuitously, do not wish to be at heavy loss by their efforts in issuing such works; and as discretion must be exercised in undertaking them, substantial aid will be required to permit their publication at any but prices which would place them beyond the reach of students and the great bulk of the people.

More general interest would be taken in the study of the language if emulation were duly encouraged, which, considering the times we live in, cannot successfully be done without substantial inducement. For this, as well as for the cheap publications, aid is required. The Gaelic Union purposes, if funds permit, to give special prizes to encourage teachers and students of the language. Subscriptions and donations for the "GAELIC PUBLICATION AND PRIZE FUND," hereby opened, are, therefore, respectfully requested, which may be forwarded to any of the members of the Union, or to the under-mentioned address, and will be duly acknowledged. The fund is intended to be permanent, but for this year it has been decided to offer *Thirty Pounds* to be distributed as prizes amongst those students who shall obtain the highest number of marks in "Celtic" at intermediate examinations. The programme of distribution will be found on p. 5. As soon as the state of the fund permits, its scope will be extended so as to embrace also teachers and pupils of National Schools.

No avoidable expense will be incurred, but some fund must be created to prevent heavy loss in publishing Irish books at low prices, and to secure a good circulation of them, as also to provide prizes.

A new edition of *Laoidh Oisín air Thír na n-óg*, suited to the requirements of the National Board's Irish programme, and also named on the Celtic programme of the Intermediate Board, edited by Mr. D. Comyn, has been already published by the Gaelic Union.

A new edition of Book I. of Dr. Keating's *Foras Feasa air Eirinn*, by P. W. Joyce, LL.D., M.R.I.A., has also been published for the Intermediate programme.

The re-issue (in parts) of the Irish version of the "Imitation of Christ" (*Searc-leamamhain Chríost*) by the late Rev. Daniel O'Sullivan, P.P., carefully revised and edited, has reached its fourth number, and will be proceeded with without further delay by the Gaelic Union.

The first, second, and third parts of a new series of

"Lessons in Gaelic, for the use of schools and for self-instruction," by Rev. John Nolan, O.D.C., forming the "First Gaelic Book," have been published for the Union, and will be immediately followed by other parts, several of which are in press.

An Irish Phrase-Book, suited to the requirements of the National Board's Irish Programme, is being prepared for the Gaelic Union by a well-known Irish scholar, a National teacher.

The present work (*Mac-ghníomhartha Fhinn*), for the Celtic Programme of the Commissioners of Intermediate Education, has been edited by Mr. David Comyn; and another, named on the same programme (*Faghail Craoibhe Chormaic Mic Airt*), is being put through the press. The Very Rev. Canon Ulick J. Bourke, P.P., M.R.I.A.; Rev. John Nolan, O.D.C.; Mr. John Fleming, of Rathgormac, and other founders and members of the "Gaelic Union," co-operate in the work of revising and editing all the proposed publications, of which some have already appeared, and others, undertaken by various hands, are in different stages of progress, and will follow without unnecessary delay.

Communications will be attended to by, and subscriptions may be made payable to, the Treasurer, Michael Corcoran, Esq., Hibernian Bank, Dublin; any of the above-named gentlemen at their private addresses; or, at

THE GAELIC UNION,
No. 19 KILDARE-STREET, DUBLIN.

The following is the programme of the distribution of prizes made in 1880, to the amount of thirty pounds, which amount at least will be allotted each year if funds permit: ten pounds to *each Grade* (Junior, Middle, and Senior), in the following manner:—

| | |
|---|---|
| Highest number of marks | £5 |
| Next in order of merit | 3 |
| Next two in order (*each* £1) | 2 |

No student will be entitled to a prize unless he obtains a pass. The distribution will be made according to the results furnished by the Commissioners of Intermediate Education.

For the names successful in 1880, see "Lessons in Gaelic," Part III.

CONTENTS AND ANALYSIS OF THIS BOOK :—
  1. Title, p. 1, and Map to face Title.
  2. Advertisement, p. 3.
  3. Contents, &c., p 6.
  4. Preface, p. 7.
  5. Ancient Text, p. 18 to p. 44.
  6. Modern Text, p. 19 to p. 45.
  7. English translation, p. 18 to p 45.
  8. Notes, p. 46. Letter, &c.
  9. Vocabulary.

1. The piece opens. Cause of the battle of Cnucha. 3. The chiefs who took part in same. 4, 5. Summary of events in the battle. 6, 12. Poetic recapitulation. 13. Birth of Deimne (Fionn). 14. He is brought for safety to Sliabh Bladhma. 15. His mother visits him after six years. 18. He is fitted to lead the chase. 19. His first chase. 20. He is concealed in Sliabh g-Crot. 22. Fiagail slays Deimne's companions. 23. Deimne is released and brought back by the two heroines. 24. He goes to hurl with the youths on Magh Life, and defeats them all. 26. He is named Fionn. 27. He slays seven of the youths. 29. Drowns nine others. 30. He catches the stags for the two heroines, and hunts for them thenceforth. 32. The sons of Morna lie in wait to kill him. 33. He goes in military service to the king of Beanntraighe. 35. He goes to Cairbrighe and defeats the king there at chess. 36. The king discovers who he is, and Fionn goes to Lochan. 37. Whose daughter falls in love with Fionn. 41. He meets the enchanted pig, which he slays. 42. And brings the head to Lochan. 43. He seeks Crimall, his father's brother, in Connacht. 44. Meets the mysterious woman. 47. He slays the warrior who killed her son, and discovers him to be the man who wounded Cumhall, his father. 48. Fionn meets with Crimall and relates his adventures. 50. He goes to study literature and poetry with Finneigeas on the Boyne, to whom it had been prophesied that Fionn should eat the salmon of knowledge. 52. The salmon is caught and given to Fionn to roast. 53. He burns his thumb with the salmon, puts the thumb in his mouth, and so fulfilling the prophecy he obtains the gift of knowledge. 55. He learns the art of poetry and composes his lay, thus proving his qualifications.

# PREFACE.

As the work lately published for the Gaelic Union is the most modern specimen of Ossianic literature, so the present tract is perhaps the most ancient that has come down to our times in what may be fairly considered something very close to its original form. It was first printed in the fourth volume of the "Ossianic Society Transactions," being edited by Dr. O'Donovan. His valuable letter, prefixed to the tract in that volume,* fully explains its history. The manuscript from which it is taken, though not among the most ancient, is accurately and faithfully copied from older manuscripts, or possibly from the veritable original. We may, therefore, fairly hold this fragment (for it is no more) to be of a date about the sixth or seventh century—we should be inclined to say even earlier. The quaint simplicity of the narrative, the many obsolete words and archaic forms, the freshness of the style, and the absence of any allusion to the existence of Christianity in Ireland or to any customs which would point out familiar intercourse with foreign nations, such as we find in almost every other "Ossianic" legend, together with the fact of no word or idea but the most primitive being introduced, would seem to carry it back to the days before the New Faith had

* See notes to end of this book.

supplanted the worship of the Sidhe and of the heavenly host, and before a new civilisation had been engrafted on the indigenous development of the native intellect under such light as Druidism had afforded, and which fusion produced the great effects we read of afterwards in the "Golden Age of Eire."

The great manuscript volumes which still exist, bearing to our day all we can know with certainty of our ancient mythology, romances, poems, tragedies, pedigrees, and chronicles, and the writings of our early Christian teachers—works such as the Leabhar Breac, Leabhar na h-Uidhre, Leabhar Laighneach, Book of Armagh, Book of Hymns, the copy of portion of Saltair Chaisil, which contains the present tract, &c.—were themselves actually written at various dates between five hundred and a thousand years ago on the identical vellum we now behold. They were compiled for the use of kings, for colleges and monasteries, and by men whose hereditary office it was to prepare accurately such compilations. When, therefore, in these manuscripts, a piece is stated to be of a certain date, or as being composed by a person from the mention of whose name we can ascertain the date at which he flourished, we may consider that it is actually of that period and by the writer named, on as good evidence as we have of the date and authorship of the Greek and Latin classics. In no one instance have we now in existence the actual autograph of any of the great books of Greece or Rome, nor even of the Sacred Writings themselves. The oldest copies we have of any of these are still but *copies;* and, in most instances, a gap of many ages separates the period of their being copied from the date of the actual composition of the original. Yet no person doubts that all these are actually as old as they are asserted to be: their style proves it, we have the evidence of history on the subject, and that of other works of later date referring to, elucidating, or augmenting the more ancient tomes; we have the evidence of analysis and exegesis by which the smallest flaw would be detected, and any appearance of anachronism prove fatal to the claims of the work. We can obtain the same evidences as to the age of the ancient Gaelic classical works. We see the statement of grave, reverend, and learned men who prepared the copies we still have the good fortune to possess; we have the internal evidence of the compositions, which suffices to prove that they belong to the remote past, to a period long antecedent to the actual date when the copyist or compiler flourished. We have the testimony both of contemporary and succeeding writers, the evidence of history and tradition, the evidence of the language itself, which, in many remarkable instances, had become obsolete and obscure when the writers of the eleventh and twelfth centuries were copying the ancient books, insomuch that they and their successors to the fourteenth and fifteenth century attached glosses and explanations in a style suited to their age, which glosses have in turn become obscure to us, moderns, their humble imitators.

Following the example of these glossographers, we have in the present edition introduced, side by side with the ancient text, a modern Irish version in the style of the present living language of our country, as well with a view to assist the student, as to show that the difference between ancient and modern Irish is, for the most part, on the surface, and is not nearly so great as is endeavoured to be proven by some who, while admitting the importance and interest of ancient Celtic remains, decry the **modern** language of Éire as unworthy of any attention. This difference, often magnified unreasonably, is **no** greater between ancient and **modern Gaelic than** between the older forms of **any modern language and** the present vernacular; **except, of course, in old** works of a technical **character, which** present great difficulty in every **language.** The modern version now given will **also serve the part** filled **by** the "Ordo" to **the** celebrated **Delphin** Classics, and cannot fail **to be** useful to the student. The mere fact of the same **ideas and** the same expressions being placed before **him** in **two** different forms — in the ancient and modern text—must have its use in fixing **on** his mind, more clearly and firmly, the gist of the work. **In a** composition like the present, so peculiar **in** its style and so "flighty" **as** to present a mere outline of a great piece—in fact, but **a** mere **argument or** analysis, as might be **imagined, of a long,** semi-historical **romance—we consider this** new version more necessary than **even the** translation. For **the sake** of learners, in **our** modern Irish text, words grown obsolete have **been replaced by their** living equivalents; **but in the majority of** cases, the ancient words themselves **might be** retained even when quite obsolete, **by so modernising** their spelling as to make them seem "as they lived now." In the present state of **our language, when good** modern Irish books are **so very rare, we believe that** Irish writers would **do immense service to** our literature of the future **by drawing in this** way **from** the literature of the past, **and** presenting the great remains of antiquity in a form intelligible to Gaelic readers of our day, rather **than** by publishing only the old texts with an English translation, which takes the reader's mind completely off making any effort to master the difficulties of the original. There are no means of knowing how far transcribers of different ages past took a similar liberty with their original, without retaining the older text side by side with their copy; but, for certain, in many cases they supplied such copious glossaries as amounted almost to a rewriting of the work, and few things which have come down to us are more useful than these glossaries. To the curious and careful student this old tract now presents itself, to compare small things with great, in an ancient, a more modern, and a foreign version, like the Rosetta stone, the inscription on which was the key to the hieroglyphic chronicles of Egypt. It will help, like the mediæval "glossed editions," to point out the way, and induce earnest workers to go farther in elucidating the inedited remains, some almost Egyptian in their obscurity, as we now have them. But little has ever been done to popularise these works among Irish readers and speakers. There is nothing so sacred about our ancient writings as not to admit of allowance being made for the due development of the Gaelic tongue from one epoch to another; and it may be permitted so to treat these remains as to cast them, as it were, in the calculus of the present age, and mould them to suit a matured and perfected language. To some extent this is done, from time to time, even in modern English. Are not even the writings of Shakespeare altered, at least as to the spelling, to suit present ideas? True, the old Anglo-Saxon remains are not treated in the way we speak of here, but they belong practically to a different language. Ancient Saxon is one speech, English is another; whereas the Gaelic of St. Patrick's time is the Gaelic of to-day, allowing for its growth from youth to maturity. It might be in some sense an advantage if early Irish were distinguished from modern Irish by a different name, as clearly as "Anglo-Saxon" is from "English;" yet, as they are but one and the same language in different stages of progress, in different phases, and under different influences, the fact that this has not been done is a proof that they were never regarded as sufficiently far apart to necessitate their being so differentiated. We know that Irish a thousand years ago was not exactly what it is to-day, and sufficient remains to prove to us that a thousand, or even five hundred years before that period it was at least as different from the language then written as that language is from our present style, and as difficult then to Irish readers almost as it is at the present day. Yet they did not look back: they went with the times. And in a thousand years to come it is not very rash to believe hopefully that the Gaelic language will have further developed, and be as far beyond our day as we are beyond Oisin's. It is still vigorous, and has all the strength of a living tongue, with many marks of neglect certainly, but few of decay.

Perhaps the best explanation in a popular way of what these ancient books so often talked about are like, is, that they resemble so many common-place-books or *albums*, in which some eminent *litera-teur* of the day, like King Cormac, or Maolmhuire son of Ceileachar, would copy for his own use or for others such pieces of ancient Gaelic literature as seemed to him most worthy of being transmitted to posterity, and of which the originals were yielding to the hand of time. By such careful scholars as these and by scribes engaged for the purpose, copies of the works of early Irish writers were handed down and multiplied before the invention of printing. And after that time in Ireland the profession of the scribe was maintained to the present day; since it is comparatively very recently that the art of printing has been availed of to multiply copies of Irish authors. There is another striking difference between the system pursued by Irish writers and their copyists and that generally in vogue elsewhere, and which must be obvious to any reader, namely, that we do not hear these books cited as the works of individuals—of Oisin, of Fearghus, of Dallan, of Cormac, of Ceannfhaoladh; nay, the authors of some of the greatest works in Irish literature remain absolutely unknown. They evidently did not ambition fame in those days, and scarcely can be said to have worked for public patronage; they were content to sink their individuality and be lost in the crowd of great unknown benefactors of their species. Their works were copied, good and bad, refined or rugged as they might be, with others often very dissimilar, into one of those great books; and so authors distant almost a thousand years apart may sometimes be found side by side on one leaf of parchment. Modern scholars are able to trace the authorship of these pieces in many instances by the style, by internal evidence or allusions, or by references in our ancient chronicles; scarcely ever is the writer's name attached in the manuscript; and in this way they differ entirely from the classic writings and the early productions of other nations, and seem most to resemble the works of certain religious communities where the individual is lost sight of in the general body. So we have "Leabhar na h-Uidhre," &c. Of the authorship of the present tract, for instance, we can have no satisfactory idea; its being found in the "Saltair of Caiseal" would tell us nothing whatever in that regard.

Our translation into English also, like that of *Tir na n-óg*, shall be exactly literal, word for word, and, in this way, more useful to a learner than Dr. O'Donovan's masterly rendering, as he did not contemplate that this work would ever be used as a school text-book. We know how useful some of Professor Connellan's little books—prepared with word-for-word *interlined* translations—have been to learners for nearly fifty years. The present is almost on the same system. Translation from one language into another enriches the language into which the translation is made, in ways other than by the actual worth of the work translated. The language is rendered more copious and pliable by being, as it were, put through a process of expansion to render it more capable of transmitting clearly the ideas conceived and expressed at first in a different idiom. English has been enriched in this way from many sources. Irish is made tributary to its greatness by scholarly translations of so much (but not nearly all) of what it has to give. Irish can itself also obtain increased pliability, copiousness and power of expression by translation from other languages, but particularly by rendering available its own vast ancient literature in a modernised form; which work would at present be one of the greatest boons that could be conferred on students and the increasing Gaelic-reading public, especially those who know the language and who would value the great treasures of past ages in their native dress, when brought within their reach, more than they would any translation.

After the poems ascribed to Aimhirgin, Roighne

Filidheach, Fercheirtne, and several others who are said to have composed in Irish before our era, the fragments attributed to Fionn, the son of Cumhall, are among the earliest productions in our language. Several **stanzas and** "prophecies" **also go by his name, but are undoubtedly forgeries, though of early date.** His sons, Fearghus Finnbheoil and the more famous Oisin, were celebrated poets, and to the latter, or at least to one of the earliest of the writers who **wrote** in his name and **with his spirit, we probably owe the** following **curious fragmentary composition.**

The poems **of the writers referred to, and the** poetical fragment by **Fionn which concludes this** piece, though obscure and archaic, are **yet sufficiently** connected with the living Irish language to **warrant us in** considering them the oldest compo**sitions in any vernacular** European tongue, **as** well **as holding a** very respectable place among similar **works** in those languages which have long since ceased to live. The same remark will apply **to** our early prose compositions, which, of ancient **date, are very** numerous.

The manuscript from which the **old text is** taken **not** being available, that edited **by Dr. O'Donovan for the Ossianic Society has been used.** It would be presumption **to change in** any way **that text,** as wherever **he has ex**pressed himself satisfied the Gaelic reader may be content. Besides, this text has been specially **named** on the Intermediate programme, **and no other** reading **would** suit, nor could any material alteration be allowed. In any case, a Gaelic work is honoured by having his name associated with it. O'Donovan himself had not **the MS.** at hand but was perfectly satisfied with **the** accuracy of the transcript prepared by Rev. **Mr.** Cleaver. His valuable notes have been retained also in this publication,\* and with them many new additional notes are now given, chiefly of a nature to assist young students and suit the book for the place it is intended to fill. Though thus, from necessity, **using his text, we** have not considered ourselves **at liberty to appropriate** his translation, but ac- **knowledge the utility it, as** well as his greater **works, has been in** our various undertakings.

**Every** place referred to in this tract, as well as **all those** named **in** the celebrated historical **romance** of "**The Pursuit of Diarmuid and** Grainne," which may be placed a generation or **so** later than the "Exploits of Fionn" as to the **time of its** taking place, will be found indicated **on the map of** Ireland **in** the third century, **which ac- companies this edition.** This map was **first** arranged **by the present** writer for the **new edition** of "**Diarmuid** and Grainne," but as it was **not there utilised, the map** has **now** been **newly lithographed and the names** mentioned in the "**Exploits of Fionn**" added. **Many** other ancient **names of places are** also marked on this map, so **as to render it a** tolerably fair outline of Ireland **at that remote** period. Numerous maps are to **be met with, of** Gaul, Britain, Caledonia, &c., about **the same era,** constructed **from** ancient records **and** monuments, but though **the** early records of **Ireland are, at** least, as copious and reliable, **they have been but** seldom availed **of** in this way, **and little has been done** to give a clear idea in **a popular way of** the early topography of the **country, beyond a** few well-constructed maps pub- **lished for particular** chronicles by Dr. Reeves and

---

\* Dr. O'Donovan's original notes are marked thus—O'D. The additional notes are given without any distinguishing mark.

Dr. O'Donovan. The documents we see sent forth by English and Scotch, and, occasionally too, by Irish publishers, as early maps of Ireland are, as a general rule, ridiculous, and of no authority whatever, not having been, like those prepared for other countries, taken from the only available reliable sources.

In order to render this translation readable, while being exactly literal, the words required to bring out clearly in English the meaning of each clause, but the equivalents of which are not found in the Irish text, are given between parenthesis, thus (—); and when, in addition to this, the literal meaning requires still further to be idiomatically explained, a second version of the clause is given in italic. Where (in a few instances) a Gaelic word in the text is, owing to the requirements of idiom, superfluous in English, the translation is given in brackets, thus [—].

The original text and the modern Irish version are placed on opposite pages, the translation being given at the foot of each page. For the convenience of students, the text has been sub-divided into very short paragraphs which are numbered alike throughout for ease of reference.

## MAC-ĠNIMARTA FINN INN SO SIS.

1. Do ḟala comtinól aiġ, ocuʀ impich deabtha, im on fianaiġeċt ocuʀ im áʀd-maeʀaiġeċt Éʀenn, idiʀ Cumull mac Tʀenmóiʀ, ocuʀ Uiʀġʀenn mac Luiġech Cuiʀʀ, do Luaiġne, .i. do Coʀco Oche Cuile Chontund don Cumull fin, aiʀ ba dib-ʀide h-Uí Taiʀʀiʀġ a ṫuaṫ-ʀom [.i. ṫuaṫ] Chumuill.

2. Toʀba, inġin Eochamáin do Eʀnaib, iʀ í ba ban-cele do Chumull no co taʀd Muiʀne Muncaim. Tucad iaʀum cath Cnucha eatuʀʀa .i. itiʀ Cumull ocuʀ Uiʀġʀend.

3. Daiʀe Deaʀġ, mac Echaid Find, mic Coiʀʀʀe Ġalaiġ, mic Muiʀeadaiġ, ocuʀ a ṁac, .i. Aed, ic tabaiʀt in chatha i ʀaʀʀad Uʀġʀunn. Ainm n-aill don Daiʀe ʀin Moʀna Muncaim.

**THE YOUTHFUL EXPLOITS OF FIONN HERE BELOW.**

1. There took place a meeting of valor and a contention of disputation concerning the (chief) Fiannship and concerning the high-stewardship of Eire, between Cumhall, son of Treunmhor, and Uirgreann, son of Lughaidh Corr of the Luaighne; i.e. (one) of the Corca-oiche (a tribe of) Cuilchontuinn that Cumhall (was): for it was from these (the) Ui Tairsigh his tribe [that is the tribe of Cumhall] (branched).

## mac-ġníoṁarṫa ḟinn ann so síos.

1. Do ṫárla cóiṁṫionol ġairġe, aġuṡ iom-
arḃaiḋ caṫa um an b-ḟiannuiġeaċṫ, aġuṡ
um árd-ṁaoraċṫ eireann, iḋir Cúṁall, mac
Ṫreunṁóir, aġuṡ Uirġreann mac Luiġeaċ
Cuirr [aon] de na Luaiġniḃ; eaḋon, buḋ de
ċorca Oiċe Ċúile-Ċonṫuinn an Cúṁall rin.
Oir buḋ ḋioḃ-ṡe Uí Ṫairriġ, a ṫuaṫ -ṡan
.i. Ṫuaṫ Ċúṁaill.

2. Iṡ rí Ṫoṁba, inġean Eoċamáin de na
earnánaiḃ buḋ ḃainċéile do Ċúṁall no ġur
pór re Muireann Mún-ċaoṁ. Ṫuġaḋ, iar
rin, caṫ Ċnuċa eadorra, eaḋon iḋir Cúṁall
aġuṡ Uirġreann.

3. Do ḃí Daire Dearġ, mac Eaċaċ ḟinn,
mic Ċairbre ġalaiġ, mic Muireaḋaiġ, aġuṡ
a ṁac, Aoḋ, aġ ṫaḃairṫ an ċaṫa a b-ḟair-
raḋ Uirġrinn. Buḋ ainm eile do'n Daire
rin Mórna Mún-ċaoṁ.

2. Torba, daughter of Eochaman of (the) Ernaans [it is she] was wife to Cumhall until he took
Muireann Múnchaomh (to wife). (The) battle of
Cnucha was given (*fought*) afterwards between
them, i.e., between Cumhall and Uirgreann.

3. Daire (the) red, **son of** Eochaidh (the) fair,
son of Cairbre (the) valiant, **son** of Muireadhach,
and his son [i.e.] Aodh, (were) giving (*fighting*) of
the battle in (the) company of (*on the side of*)
Uirgreann. Another name for that Daire (was)
Morna (of the) fair-neck.

4. Do beṗaṙ iaṙum in caṫ iaṙ ṙin; do ṗala iteṙ Luicet ocuṙ Aeḋ mac Moṙna, iṙ in caṫ; ꞅonaṙ Luicet Aeḋ co ṗoṙ mill a leṫ-ṙoṙc, coniḋ de ṙo lil a ainm Goll ó ṙin i le e.

5. Do tuit Lucet la Goll; ꞅonaṙ ḋan ṙeṙ coiméta coṙṙ-builꞅ a ṙét ṙeiṙin Cumull iṙ in caṫ. Do tuit Cumull la Goll mac Moṙna iṙ in caṫ, ocuṙ beiṙiḋ a ṙoiḋb ocuṙ a cenḋ leiṙ, coniḋ de ṙin bui ṙiċ bunaḋ itiṙ Finn ocuṙ mac Moṙna, coniḋ de ṙin ṙo cet in ṙeanċaiḋ :—

6. Goll mac Daṙe Deiṙꞅ co m-blaiḋ
Mic Eċaiḋ ṙinn,—ṙinn a ꞅail,
Mic Caiṙṙṙe ꞅalaiḋ co n-ꞅail,
Mic Muiṙeaḋaiꞅ a Finḋmaiꞅ.

7. Ro maṙb Goll Luicet na ceḋ,
A caṫ Cnuċa, noċa bṙec,
Luicet ṙinn in ꞅaiṙceḋ ꞅlain
La mac Moṙna ḋo ṙoċaiṙ.

8. Iṙ leiṙ ḋo tuit Cumull móṙ,
I caṫ Cnuċa na caṫ-ṙloꞅ

2⟨1⟩0 A.D.

4. The battle [indeed] is fought after that; (a single fight) took place between Luichet and Aodh, son of Morna, in the battle ; Luichet wounds Aodh, so (that he) destroyed one of his eyes, [*lit.* his half-eye,] so from it his name Goll followed him from that forth.

5. Luichet fell by Goll. The keeper of his own round-bag of jewels (*treasure-bag*) wounds Cumhall [then,] in the battle. Cumhall fell by Goll, son of Morna in the battle: and (Goll) brings his arms and his head with him, so from that there was a settled hatred between Fionn (son of Cum-

4. Tugaḋ iaraṁ an caṫ iar ṡin. Do ṫárla cómrac roiṁ Luiċet agur Aoḋ mac Móṙna annr an g-caṫ; gonar Luiċet Aoḋ gur ṁill re a leaṫ-ṡúil, gur ṫé rin do lean a ainm Goll ó rin a leiṫ ḋé.

5. Do ṫuit Luiċet le Goll. Gonar rear-cóiṁeuda corr-boilg a reoḋ réin Cúṁall annr an g-caṫ. Do ṫuit Cúṁall le Goll mac Móṙna annr an g-caṫ; agur beirear Goll a éide agur a ċeann leir; gur ṫé rin bí ruaṫ buan roir Fionn mac Cúṁaill agur Goll mac Móṙna. Go ṫé rin do ċan an reanċaiḋe:—

6. Buḋ h-é Goll mac Daire ḋeirg clúṁair mic Eaċaċ finn—dob' fionn a ġal; mic Cairbre galaig an ġail mic Muireaḋaig ó Fionn-ṁáġ.

7. Do ṁarb Goll Luiċet na g-céad, a g-caṫ Cnuca, ní breug é: do ṫrargraḋ Luiċet fionn an ġairgiḋ ġlain le mac Móṙna.

8. Ir leir do ṫuit Cúṁall mór, a g-caṫ Cnuca na g-caṫ-ṡluaġ: ráṫ do ṫug riaḋ an

hall) and (Goll) **son of Morna**. So from that sang the historian:—

6. Goll (was) son of Daire (the) red of fame, (*famous*) (who was) son of Eochaidh (the) fair, fair (was) his valour, son of Cairbre (the) valiant (famous) of prowess, **son of** Muireadhach from Fionnmhagh.

7. Goll slew Luichet of hundreds, in **the** battle of Cnucha, **no** lie (is this); Luichet the fair of the pure valour, by (the) **son** of Morna **was** slain.

8. It is by him fell Cumhall (the) great, in the battle of Cnucha of **the** battle-hosts; the cause

Aipe tuc-pat in cath tenv,
Im pianaiveét na h-Epenv.
9. batap clanva Mópna ip in cath,
Ocup Luaigni na Tempach,
Aip ba leo pianup pep Fáil,
Ppia laim caé pig co po-baig.
10. buí mac ac Cumull co m-buaiv—
In Finn puilech paebup cpuaiv.
Finn ocup Goll mór a m-blav,
Trén vo ponnpatap cogav.
11. Iap pin vo ponnpatap pív,
Finv ocup Goll na céo n-gním,
Co topcuip banb Sinna ve,
Fa'n muicc a Temuip Luaicpe.
12. Aev ba h-ainm vo mac Daipe,
Cop gaev luicet con aine,
O po gaet mac Luaigne lonv,
Daipe conpuitea pip Goll. g.
13. Toppach po accaib Cumull a mnai .i.
Muipne, ocup beipiv pi mac, ocup bepa ainm
vo, .i. Demne. Tic Fiaccail mac Concinn
ocup bovhmall, ban-vpai, ocup in liath Lua-

(for which) they fought the vigorous battle (was) concerning the Fiannship of Eire.

9. The children of Morna were in the battle, and the Luaighne of Teamhair; for it was with them (*theirs was*) the Fiannship of (the) men of (Inis) Fail by the hand of each king of great power.

10. (There) was a son to Cumhall of victories (*the victorious*)—the blood-shedding Fionn of hard weapons. Fionn and Goll, great (was) their fame, brave(ly) they made war.

11. After that they made peace—Fionn and

cat teann, do bí um ḟiannuiġeact na h-Éi-
ṗeann.

9. Do biḋeadaṗ Clanna Mórna annṗ an
g-cat, aguṗ Luaiġne na Teamṗac; óiṗ buḋ
leo-ṗan ḟiannuiġeact ṗeaṗ Inṗe-ṗáil, le
láiṁ ġac ṗiġ go ṗó-ṫṗeun.

10. Do bí mac ag Cúṁall na m-buaiḋ—
Ḟionn ṗuilteac, ṗaoḃaṗ-ċṗuaiḋ. Ḟionn aguṗ
Goll, buḋ ṁóṗ a g-clú, go tṗeun do ṗinn-
eadaṗ cogaḋ.

11. Iaṗ ṗin do ṗinneadaṗ ṗioc—Ḟionn aguṗ
Goll na g-céad gníoṁ—guṗ tṗaṗgṗaḋ
banḃ Sionna ḋé aiṗ an máġ a d-Teaṁaiṗ
Luacṗa.

12. Aoḋ buḋ ainm do ṁac Daiṗe guṗ
ġoin Luicet é le bṗiġ: ó do ġoin mac Luaiġne dána é, tugaḋ Goll dó maṗ ainm.

13. D'ḟág Cúṁall a bean toṗṗac, eaḋon
Muiṗeann, aguṗ beiṗeaṗ ṗi mac, aguṗ beiṗ ṗi
ainm dó, Deimne. Tig Ḟiacail mac Ċunciṅn
aguṗ Bóḋṁall, ban-dṗaoi, aguṗ Liat Luacṗa

Goll of the hundreds of exploits—till was slain
Banbh Sionna (in consequence) of that (peace)
under (*on*) the plain at Teamhair Luachra.

12. Aodh was (the) name to (the) son of Daire,
till Luichet wounded him with agility; since (the)
bold son of Luaighne wounded (him) Goll was
given him (as a name).

13. Cumhall left pregnant his wife [i.e.] Muireann, and she bears a son, and she gives a name
to him [i.e.] Deimne. Fiacail son of Cucheann
and Bodhmhall the Druidess, and [the] Liath
Luachra come to visit Muireann, and they take

cṗa ꝺo ṗaiɼeꝺ Muiṗne, oċuṗ beiṗiꝺ leo in
mac, aiṗ niṗ lam a máṫaiṗ a ḃeṫ aicce.
Fuiꝺiṗ Muiṗne la Ɣleoiṗ Lám-ꝺeṗɼ, la ṗi
Lampṗaiɼe iaṗꝺam, coni ꝺe-ṗiꝺe in ṗaꝺ, Finn
mac Ɣleoiṗ.
14. Luiꝺ́ cṗa ḃoꝺhmall oċuṗ in Liaṫ,
oċuṗ in mac leo i ṗoiṫṗuib Sleiḃi ḃlaꝺma.
Ro h-ailleꝺ in mac anꝺ ṗin i ṫaiꝺe. ꝺeiṫḃiṗ
on, aiṗ ba h-imꝺa ɼilla ṫailċaiṗ ṫinneṗnaċ,
oċuṗ laech neimneċh naimꝺiɼe, oċuṗ ṗeiniꝺ
ṗeṗɼaċh ṗuiṫhnuṗach ꝺo Laeċpiꝺ Luaiɼne,
oċuṗ ꝺo maċaiḃ Moṗna ṗoṗ ti in mic ṗin,
—oċuṗ Tulċa mic Cumuill. Ro ail-ṗeṫ iaṗum
in ꝺá banṗeinꝺiɼ ṗin ṗṗi ṗé ṗoꝺa é ṗan
ṗamlaiꝺ́ ṗin.

15. Tic a máṫaiṗ a cinꝺ ṗé m-ḃliaꝺan iaṗ
ṗin ꝺ'ṗiṗ a mic, aiṗ ꝺo h-innṗiꝺ ꝺi a ḃeṫ iṗ
in inaꝺ uṫ, oċuṗ ṗo ba h-ecail le mac Moṗna
ꝺo.

16. Ciꝺ ṫṗaċṫ, aṫṗaċṫ aṗ caċ ṗaṗach i n-a
céle, co ṗáinicc ṗoiṫṗib Sleḃe ḃlaꝺma; ṗo-

(away) with them the son, for his mother dared
not (risk) him to be with her. Muireann marries
with Gleoir of the red hands, [with] king of
Lamhraighe afterwards, so from that the saying,
Fionn son of Gleoir.

14. Meantime Bodhmhall and [the] Liath and
the son with them, go into the wilds of Sliabh
Bladhma. The son was reared there in concealment. Necessity, indeed (was for this), for (there)
was many a sturdy strong-ribbed fellow, and
venomous hostile warrior, and angry, morose
hero of (the) warriors of Luaighne, and of (the)

ᴅ'ionnʀuiᴅe Muiʀne, aᵹuʀ beiʀɪᴅ leo an mac, óiʀ níoʀ lám a máᴛaiʀ é ᴅo beiᴛ aici. ᴘó-ʀaiᴅ Muiʀeann le Gleoiʀ láimᴅeaʀᵹ, ɪuᵹ lámʀaiᵹe iaʀ ʀin: ᵹuʀ ᴅé ʀin ᴛiᵹ an ʀáᴅ, ꝼionn mac Gleoiʀ.

14. Tʀáᴛ ᴛeiᴅ bóᴅmall aᵹuʀ liaᴛ aᵹuʀ an mac a ᵹ-cóimᴅeaᴄᴛ leo a b-ꝼáʀacaib Sléibe bláma. ᴅo h-oileaᴅ an mac ann ʀin a b-ʀolaᴄ. ᴅo bí eiᵹean ᵹo ᴅeimin óiʀ buᴅ iomᴅa ᵹiolla láiᴅiʀi, ᴛeann-aʀnaᴄ, aᵹuʀ laoᴄ nimneaᴄ námaᴅaᴄ, aᵹuʀ ꝼiann ꝼeaʀᵹaᴄ ᴅoiʀb ᴅe laoᴄʀaiᴅ luaiᵹne, aᵹuʀ ᴅe macaib Móʀna, aᵹuʀ Tulᴄa mac Cúmaill maʀ an ᵹ-ceuᴅna, aiʀ ᴛí an mic ʀin. Gíᴅeaᴅ, ᴅ'oil an ᴅá bain-ꝼéinniᴅe ʀin é ꝼaoi an ᴛ-ʀámail ʀin le ʀé ꝼaᴅa.

15. Tiᵹ a máᴛaiʀ a ᵹ-ceann ʀé m-bliaᴅain iaʀ ʀin ᴅ'ꝼioʀ a mic, óiʀ ᴅo h-innʀeaᴅ ᴅí é beiᴛ annʀ an ionaᴅ úᴅ: aᵹuʀ buᴅ eaᵹal léi mac Móʀna ᴅó.

16. Ciᴅ ᴛʀáᴄᴛ, ᴅ'eiʀiᵹ ʀi aʀᵹaᴄ ꝼáʀaᴄ ann a ᴄéile, ᵹo ʀainic ʀi ꝼáʀaiᵹe Sléibe

sons of Morna on design of (*in wait for*) that son, (*boy*) and Tulcha, son of Cumhall (likewise seeking to destroy him.) However, [they] those two heroines reared him during a long time under (*after*) that manner.

15. His mother comes at (the) head (*end*) of six years after that to knowledge of (*to visit*) her son, for (it) was told [to] her his being in that place (*that he was, &c.*), and there was fear with her (the) son of Morna for him. (*She feared the son of Morna on his account.*)

16. What narration (is needed further)— she) went out of each desert into its fellow

geib in fian-boith ocuf in mac i n-a coolao
innti, ocuf toccbaio fi an mac i n-a h-ucht
iafoain, ocuf timfaige fria he, ocuf fi trom
iafum.

17. Conio ano fin oo rom na fanna ic
muifin im a mac—
Coosil fe fuanán fáime, [ocuf af oile].

18. Timnaf an ingin celebfao oo na ban-
feinoéouib iaf fin, ocuf atbeft friu nom
gaboair in mac co mao in-feinéoa é, ocuf
fo forbaö in mac iaf fin cuf ba h-in-felga é.

19. Tainic in mac i n-a aenuf imach in
afaile lá ano, ocuf io conoaifc [in pfaf
lacha co] n-a lachain foff in loc. Taf-
laic ufchuf fuithib ocuf fo teftaif a finn-
fao ocuf a h-eteoa oi, co tocuif tam-nell
fuiffe, ocuf fo gab-fam iafum, ocuf fof tuc
leif oo chum na fian-boithi. Conio hi fin
ceo fealg Fino.

(*from one to the other*), till (she) reached (the)
wilds of Sliabh Bladhma: (she) found the
hunting-booth, and the son in his sleep (*asleep*) in
it (*therein*); and she lifts the son in her bosom
afterwards, and (she) gathers him to her (*presses
him to her bosom*), and she heavy (*she being pregnant*)
then (*at the time*).

17. So then (she) made (*composed*) the (*these*)
verses caressing [about] her son—
"Sleep with (the) slumber of pleasure," *et re-
liqua*: (*qui desunt*).

18. The daughter (*woman*) bids farewell to the
heroines after that, and speaks with them (*asks
them*) would they not take (charge of) the son

bláoṁa; ruaip pí an piann-boṫ aguy an mac 'na coolaṁ imṫi: agup tógaiṁ pí an mac 'na h-uċt aip pin, agup páipgiṁ pí léi é, agup pí tpom an tan pin.

17. Leip pin oo ṗinne pí na paimn po ag múipneaċt a mic—Covail le puanán páṁ,—agup an cuio eile.

18. Ceileabpap an bean oo na bainpéinniṁiḃ iap pin, agup labpap leo [.i. pappuigeap oíoḃ] an ngabvaoip an mac go m-baṁ in-péinneaṁa é : agup oo coṫuigeaṁ an mac iap pin gup ab in-peilge é.

19. Táinic an mac 'na aonap amaċ lá eile ann, agup oo ċonnaipc pe an ppaplaċa agup a lacain aip an loċ. Oo ċuip pe upċup púta, agup oo geapp pe a cleitiṁe agup a h-eiteaṁa ṁí, go páinic taiṁ-neull aippi, agup oo gaḃ pe í iap pin, agup oo tug pe leip í cum na piann-boiṫe. Gup ab í pin an ċeuo pealg Ḟinn.

(*boy*) till he should be fit for **the** Fiann (*of age fit to take rank among the Fiann*); and the son was reared after that (by them) till he was fit for chase (*fitted to conduct the chase*).

19. The **son** (*Fionn*) came in his oneship (i.e. *alone, by himself*) forth in another day **there** (*a certain day*), and saw the duck with the (young) ducks upon the lake. (He) threw a cast under (*at*) them, and cut her feathers and her wings off her till there came a **death-trance on** her (*so that she died*); and he **took** (her) after, and (he) brought (her) with him unto the hunting-booth. So that is (the) first chase of Fionn.

20. Luid-rium la ser cespda iaptain for
techeu mac Morna ; co m-boi fo Crottaib
accu.  Ite a n-anmanda-rde, Futh ocur
Ruth ocur Regna Maṁ-Feda, ocur Temle,
ocur Oilpe, ocur Rogein.

21. Tainiġ im buile tairirim and rin, co
n-derna carrach de, conid de do ġairtea
Deimne mael de.
22. Bi foġlaid a Laigen in tan rin .i. Fiaccail mac Coṁna e-ride. Do rala din Fiaccail
i Fid Ġaible forr an ser ceardai, ocur ro
marb uili act Deimne n- a senur ; bui rum ac
Fiaccail mac Coṁna iar rin i n- a tiġ, a fer-
cinn uairbeoil.

23. Teccait in dá ban-féinoiġ bu dear co
tech Fiacla mic Coṁnai, for iarr Deimne,
ocur do berar doib é ; ocur do berait leo a
n-der hé iartam cur in innad cedna.

24. Do chuaid-rom lá aile and a senar

20. He went with folk of trade (*certain artificers*) afterwards in flight (because) of (the) **sons** of Morna ; so he was under (*about*) the Crotta (*Gailte, Galtees*) with **them** (in concealment). It is (**these** are) their **names** : Futh and Ruth and Regna of Magh Feadha, and Teimle, and Oilpe and Roigein.
21. Blisters **came** over him there, so that (there) **was** made of **him a** bald-head (*or one affected with cutaneous disease*), **so from** that Deimne (the) bald used to be called **to** him.
22. (There) **was a** plunderer in Leinster (at)

20. Cuaiḋ ṗe maille le aoṗ céiṗoc eiṡin iaṗ ṗin aiṗ ceiċeaḋ, maṗ ġeall aiṗ macaiḃ Móṗna ṡo m-biḋeaḋ ṗe timċioll Sleiḃe ṡ-Cṗoc maṗ aon leo. Iṗ ṗiaḋ a n-anmanna-ṗan :—Fuṫ aṡuṗ Ruṫ aṡuṗ Reṡna Maiġe Feaḋa, aṡuṗ Ceimle, aṡuṗ Oilpe aṡuṗ Roiṡein.

21. Ṫáinic bolṡaiġe ṫaiṗuṗ-ṗean ann ṗin, ṡo n-ḋeaṗnaḋ caiṗṗaċ ḋé, ṡuṗ ab ó'n niḋ ṗin ḋo ṡaiṗṫí Deimne maol ḋé.

22. Do ḃí ṗoġlaiḋe a Laiġean an can ṗin, eaḋon, Fiaṡail mac Cóḋna éiṗean. Do ṫáṗla ann ṗin Fiaṡail a b-Fioḋ-ṡaiḃle aiṗ an aoṗ céiṗḋe, aṡuṗ ḋo ṁaṗḃ ṗe iaḋ uile aċc Deimne 'na aonaṗ: ḋo ḃí ṗe a ṡ-coiṁḋeaċt le Fiaṡail mac Cóḋna iaṗ ṗin ann a ṫiġ a ṗeiṗcinn ṗuaiṗ.

23. Ciṡiḋ an ḋáḃain-ḟéinniḋe ó ḋeaṗ ṡo ciġ Fiaṡla mic Cóḋna, aiṗ iaṗṗaiḋ Deimne, aṡuṗ beiṗiṫeaṗ ḋóiḃ é; aṡuṗ beiṗiḋ leo a n-ḋeaṗ é, iaṗ ṗin, ṡuṗ an ionaḋ ceuḋna, ann a ṗaiḃ ṗe ṗoiṁe ṗin.

24. Do ċuaiḋ ṗe, lá eile, 'na aonaṗ amaċ

that time, namely, Fiagail son of Codna [was he]. Then Fiagail chanced (to come) in Fiodh Gaibhle upon the artificers, and slew all **but** Deimne in his oneship (*alone*): he was (*remained*) **with** Fiagail **son** of Codna in his house **in** a cold marsh.

23. The two heroines come southward to (the) **house of** Fiagail, **son** of Codna, in search (of) **Deimne, and** he is given **to** them; and they take **with them** from the south **him,** afterwards, to the same place (as before).

24. He went another day in his oneship (*alone*) forth, till he reached (the) plain of Life (*Liffey*), to

amach co ṁacht Maġ Liḟe ġo aroile dún ann, co nor ḟaccaiḋ in macraiḋ óg oc imáin ḟor ḟaiċe in' dúine. Tic-rum com luḋ no com imáin ḟriu-rum.

25. Tic iar n-a báraċ ocur do beirt ceṫraime i n-a aġaiḋ; ticit arír a triar i n-a aġaiḋ. Cid tráct, iatnaġat uile i n-a aġaiḋ/ ra deoiġ, ocur do bered-rum leṫ cluiċe forra uili.

26. Cia h-ainm ril ḟort? ol riat. Deimne, ol re. Inniriḋ in macraiḋ d'ḟir in dúnaiḋ in ní rin. Mairbaiḋ-rideé mad contuicti, mar a cumactaċi é, ol re. Ni caemramair ní do, ol riat; cur ab Deimne a ainm. Cindar a h-eccorc, ol re. Macaem tuctach, ḟind, ol riat. Ir ainm do Deimne Find amlaiḋ rin, ol re-ream. Conid de rin aubertir in macraiḋ ḟri-rum Finn.

27. Tic-rum iar n-a báraċ dia raiġid, ocur luid cuccu i n-a cluiċi ḟo certat a lorġa ḟair an aen ḟect. Imaraim ruiċib-

another (certain) fortress there till he saw the [young] youth (of the place) hurling on the lawn of the fortress. He comes to exercise or to hurl with them.

25. He comes after (*on*) the morrow, and they send a fourth (of their number) in his face (*against him*): they come again, the third (of their number *once more*) against him. What (need of further) discourse,—they go all against him at last, and he gives (*wins*) a half game on them all.

26. What name is on thee? said they. Deimne, said he. The youths tell the man (*owner*) of the

go ṗáinic ṙe Máġ Liṙe go ḋún eiḷe ann, go b-ṙacaiḋ ṙe an macṙaiḋ óg (na h-áite ṙin) ag iomáin aiṙ ṙaiṫċe an ḋúin. Cig ṙe ag imiṙt no ag iomáin ḷeo-ṙan.

25. Cig ṙe iaṙ n-a máṙaċ, agus beiṙiḋ cea-ṫṙama ḋ'a n-aiṙeaṁ 'na aġaiḋ: tigiḋ aniṙ a ḋ-tṙian 'na aġaiḋ. Ciḋ tṙáċt, ḋ'eiṙ-ġeaḋaṙ uiḷe 'na aġaiḋ ṙá ḋeoig, agus beiṙiḋ ṙe ḷeaṫ cluiċe oṙṙa uiḷe.

26. Ca h-ainm a tá oṙt? aṙ ṙiaḋ. Ḋeimne, aṙ ṙe. Innṙiḋ an macṙaiḋ ḋ' ṙeaṙ an ḋúin an niḋ ṙin. Maṙbaiḋ-ṙe é, má tig ṙe aniṙ, má tá ṙe ann buṙ g-cúmaċt, aṙ ṙe. Ní ṙeuḋamuiḋ niḋ a ḋeunaḋ ḷeiṙ, aṙ ṙiaḋ: guṙ ab Ḋeimne a ainm. Ciannos a tá a ċuma? aṙ ṙe. Macaoṁ ḋeaġ-ċumta, ṙionn, aṙ ṙiaḋ. Is ainm do Ḋeimne Fionn aṁlaiḋ ṙin, aṙ ṙeiṙean. Is uime ṙin, ḋo ġaiṙḋíṙ an macṙaiḋ Fionn ḷeiṙ-ṙean.

27. Cig ṙe iaṙ n-a máṙaċ ḋ'a n-ionnsuiḋe, agus cuaiḋ ċuca ann a g-cluiċe: ḋo ċuiṙea-ḋaṙ a loṙga ḋ'uṙċuṙ aiṙ a n-aoin-ṙeaċt.

fortress that thing. Kill ye him if he comes (again) if ye can, said he. We cannot (do) any-thing to him, said they: Deimne is his name. What **manner** (is) his appearance? said he. A fair, shapely lad, said they. It is a name for Deimne Fionn, like that (*Deimne* **shall** *be called* **Fionn**, fair, *on that account*), said *he*. So from that **the youths** used to say with him (*name him*) Fionn.

27. **He comes** (again) after the morrow (i.e., **the next day**) to their meeting (*to them*), and went towards them in their game: they aimed their

rium, ocuṛtṛaṛcṛaiṫ moṛṛeiṛiṛ ṫib. Luiṫ
uatḣib a ṛoitḣṛuib Slebe Blaṫma.

28. Tic iaṛium i cḣinṫ ṛeċtmuine iaṛ ṛin,
cuṛ in m-baile céṫna. Iṛ amlaiṫ batuṛ in
macṛaiṫ ic ṛnaṁ ṛoṛṛ in loch bi i n- a ṛoṛṛaṫ.
Ṡṛennaiṡit in macṛaiṫ e-ṛium imteċht ṫim-
baṫa ṛṛiu.

29. Linṡiṫ-ṛin iṛ in loch cuca iaṛ ṛin, ocuṛ
báṫiṫ nonbuṛ ṫib ṛo'n loch, ocuṛ téit ṛéin
ṛa Sliab Blaṫma iaṛ ṛin. Cia ṛo báiṫ in
macṛaiṫ, ol caċh. Finn, ol ṛiat; conaṫ
aṛ ṛin ṛo leanaṫ Finn e.

30. Tic-ṛium ṛeċt anṫ taṛ Sliab Blaṫma
amach, ocuṛ in ṫa ban-ṛénṫiṫ i maille ṛṛiṛ;
conacaṛ alma imṫicṛcṛiṛ ṫ'aṡaib alluiṫ ṛo-
ṛaiṛ in ṛlébe.

31. Mo nuaṛ tṛia,! oṛ in ṫa ṛen-tuinn, ní
tic ṫinn aṛtuṫ neich ṫib ṛúṫ accainn. Tic
ṫim-ṛa, [ol Finn] ocuṛ ṛitḣaiṫ ṛoṛṛio, ocuṛ
aṛtaiṫ ṫá n-aṡ ṫib, ocuṛ beiṛiṫ leiṛ ṫia

staves on him together. *He* aims at them, and
slaughters (a big six) *seven* of them. (He) went
from them (then) in the wilds of Sliabh Bladhma.
28. (He) comes, indeed, at (the) head (*end*)
of a week after that to the same place. It is thus
were the youths (then engaged)—swimming on
the lake (which) was in their neighbourhood. The
youths defy him (to) come to swim with them.
29. He plunges in the lake towards them after
that, and (he) drowns nine of them under the
lake, and goes himself under (*towards*) Sliabh

Aimpigear rúta-ran, agur trargnaiv re móirreiream víob. Cuaiv re uata ann rin go rárataib Sléibe bládma.

28. Tig re, umorro, a g-ceann rea-ćtmaine iar rin gur an m-baile ceuona. Ir amlaiv vo bívearar an macraiv, eavon, ag rnám air an loć vo bí 'na b-rarrav. Greannuigiv an macraiv éirean teaċt ag rnám mar aon leo.

29. Lingiv re annr an loć cuca iar rin, agur báivrv re naonbar víob ra'n loć, agur teiv re réin go Sliab bládma iar rin. Cia h-é vo báiv an macraiv? ar caċ. Fionn, ar rav v' ran beo. Mar ro, ar rin vo lean an t-ainm Fionn vé.

30. Tig re tráċ tar Sliab bládma amać, agur an vá bain-féinniče a maille leir: go b-racavar ealta rár-lúćmar v'riavaib allta v'rárać an t-rléibe.

31. Mo nuar trá! ar an vá rean-vuine, ní tig linn aon ćeann víob rúv v'rartugav againn. Tig liom-ra, ar Fionn, agur mèiv re orra, agur rartuigiv vá riav víob, agur

Bladhma after that. Who drowned the youths? said all. Fionn, said they (who survived.) So from that (the name) Fionn followed him.

30. He **came a** time then over Sliabh Bladhma out, and **the two** heroines in company with him: they saw **a** very nimble drove of wild deer [*or cows*] (of the) forest of the mountain.

31. My woe indeed! (*or alas!*) said the two old people (*women*), it comes not of (*with*) us (*we cannot*) retain one of these yonder with us. It comes of (*with*) myself, (*I can*) said Fionn, and (he) runs on

3

ꝼiann-boiṫ. Do gni-ꞃium ꞃelg co gnáṫaċ
dóib iaꞃ ꞃ .

32. Eiꞃiḋ buain ꝼeꞃta, a gilla, oꞃ na ban-
ꝼéneḋa ꞃinꞃ, aiꞃ ataiṫ mic Móꞃna ꝼoꞃ aicill
do maꞃbṫa.

33. Do luid-ꞃium n-a aenaꞃ uaḋib co
ꞃiaċt Loch Léin oꞃ Luaċaiꞃ, cuꞃ
aṫcuiꞃ a amꞃaine ac ꞃig Benṫꞃaige and
ꞃin; ní ꞃó ꞃloind-ꞃim iꞃ in inaḋ ꞃin he, aċt
cena, ní buí iꞃ in ꞃé ꞃin ꞃelgaiꞃe a innꞃamla.

34. Iꞃ amlaiḋ aꞃbeꞃt in ꞃí ꞃinꞃ : via ꝼacc-
baḋ Cumull mac, ol ꞃe, daꞃ lat ꞃo bo
tuꞃa é; aċt cena, ní cualamuꞃ-ne mac d'
ꝼaccbáil do aċt Tulċa mac Cumaill, ocuꞃ
atá ꞃin ac ꞃí Alban in amꞃaine.

35. Celebꞃaiḋ-ꞃim don ꞃí iaꞃ ꞃin, ocuꞃ téṫ
uaiḋ co Caiꞃbꞃige (.i. Ciaꞃꞃaige i nviu),
ocuꞃ atnuig ic in ꞃig ꞃin a n-amꞃaine. Tic
in ꞃí iaꞃum ac ꞃrocellaċt in aꞃaile ló. Te-
coiꞃgid-ꞃim laiꞃ ocuꞃ beꞃid ꞃeċt cluiċi
diaig aꞃaile.

them, and retains two **deer of** them, and **brings**
them, with him to his hunting-booth.  He used **to
make** chase constantly for them after that.

32. Go from us henceforth, O youth, said the
**heroines** with (*to*) him; **for** the sons of Morna
**are on watch (for) thy** killing, (*to kill thee*).

33. He went in his oneship (*alone*) from them
till (he) reached Loch Léin, over Luachair,
till he gave up (*hired*) his (military) services to
(the) King of Beanntraighe then : they surnamed
him not in that place, howbeit (there) was not **in
that** time a hunter of his like (*his equal*).

beiriú re leir iao o'a fiann-boit. Do ġní-
ṫeaú re realġ ġo ġnátać ṫóib iar rin.

32. Eiriġ uainn rearoa, a ġiolla, ar na
bain-féinniṫe leir, óir táio mic Mórna air
tí oo ṁaribta.

33. Do ćuaiṫ re 'na aonar uaċa ġo ráinic
re Loć Léin, ór Luaċair, ġur aċċuir re
a aṁraine aġ riġ Beannċiaiġe ann rin:
níor floinn riao é annr an ionao rin, aċt
ceana, ní raib annr an am rin realġaire a
ionnráṁla.

34. Ir aṁlaiú ro ṫeir an riġ leir: oá
b-fáġbaú Cúṁall mac, ar re, oar liom ġur
ab tura é, aċt ceana, ní ćualamar-ne mac
o'fáġbáil oó, aċt Tulća mac Cúṁaill, aġur
tá reirean aġ riġ Albann a n-aṁraine.

35. Ceileabrar Fionn oo'n riġ iar rin,
aġur teiṫ re uaiṫ ġo Cairbriġe, eaṫon
Ciarraiṫe a n-oiu, aġur fanaiú re aġ an riġ
rin a n-aṁraine. Tiġ an riġ iar rin aġ
fićeallaċt lá eiġin. Imriú re leir aġur
beir re reaċt ġ-cluiċċe oiaiġ a n-oiaiġ.

34. **It is thus says the** king to him: if Cumhall (had) left **a** son, quoth he, it seems with thee (*me*) (methinks) **thou** shouldst be he; **but**, howbeit, we heard **not a son** to leave by him (*that he left a son*). but Tulcha, son of Cumhall, and that (son) is with (the) king of Scotland **in** (military) service.

35. He (*Fionn*) bids farewell to the **king after** that, and goes from him **to** Cairbrighe (i.e., Ciarraighe [*Kerry*] to-day [*now*]), and abides **with** that king in (military) service. The king comes afterwards a chess-playing a certain day. He plays with him and wins seven games after each other.

36. Cia tura? ol in rí. Mac aithig do Luaignib Tempach, ol re. Acc, ol in rí; áct ir tú in mac ror tuc Muirne do Cumall, ocur na bi runn ní ir ra, nár ut maribtar ror m'enech-ra.

37. Luid ar ian rin co Cuillind [Ó Cuanach], co teć Lochain rlait gobann: ingin ro caem lair-rde .i. Cruithne a h-ainm: adnaig ri grád do'n gilla.

38. Do bér-ra m'ingin duit, ol in goba, cin co fetar cia tu. Fóidir in ingin leir in gilla iartain.

39. Déna rleza dam, ol in gilla rir in n-gobann. Do gní din Lochan di rleig do Celeabrad dan do Lochan ocur luid reime.

40. A mic, ar Lochan, ná h-eirig ir in rlige ror a m-bi an muc dia n-ab ainm in beo; ir rí ro rarad meodon Mumun.

41. Ocur ir red tra do rala do'n gilla dul ror in rlige ror m-bi in muc. Adnaig in muc cuice iar rin. Foceird-rim dna

36. Who (art) thou? quoth the king. Son of a peasant of (the) Luaighni of Teamhair, says he. Not so, said the king; but thou art the son whom Muireann bore to Cumhall, and be (*stay*) not here longer, that (thou) mayest not be slain (whilst trusting) on my hospitality.

37. (Fionn) went out after that to Cuillean [O g-Cuanach] to (the) house of Lochan, a chief-smith: (there was) an exceeding-beautiful daughter with him: i.e., Cruithne, her name: she gave love to the youth.

38. I will give my daughter to thee, says the smith, though I know not who thou (art). The daughter then marries with the youth.

36. Cia tusa? ar an ríg. Mac aitig de Luaignib na Teampac, ar ré. Ní h-eaḋ, ar an ríg; aċt ir tu an mac mug Muirinn do Ċumall, aguir ná bí ann ro níor ria ionnor naċ muirride tu air m'éineaċ-ra.

37. Ċuaiḋ Fionn ar iar rin go Cuilleann [na g-Cuanaċ], go tig Locain plaiċ-goba: bí ingean ró-ċaoṁ aige-rean, Cruitne a h-ainm: ċug ri gráḋ do'n giolla, eaḋon d'Ḟionn.

38. Déanfad-ra m'ingean duit-re, ar an goba, giḋ ní feadar me cia tu. Pórair an ingean leir an ngiolla iar rin.

39. Deun rleaga ḋam, ar an giolla leir an ngobainn. Gníḋ Locan ḋá ṡleig ḋó ann rin. Ceileabrar Fionn ann rin do Locan aguir ċuaiḋ re roiṁe.

40. A ṁic, ar Locan, ná h-eirig annr an t-rlige air a m-biḋ an ṁuc d'a n-ab ainm an Beo: ir rí d'fáruig Meaḋon-Ṁuṁa.

41. Aguir ir eaḋ tria do tárluig do'n giolla dul air an rlige air a m-biḋ an muc. D'eirig an muc ċuige iar

39. Make spears for me, said the youth to the smith. Lochan made then two spears for him. (Fionn) takes leave then of Lochan, and went before him (*goes his way*).

40. O son, said Lochan, go not in the way on which is (usually to be seen) the pig to which is name (*which is called*) Beo (*the Living*); it is she devastated (all) middle Munster.

41. But it is it, just, that happened to the youth (to) go on the way on (which) was the pig. The pig after that went towards him (*made at him*). He put (*made*) then a cast of his spear on her, so

uscur oi ṙleiġ ḟuiṙṙu, co ṗo luid tṙíċe, co
ṗuṙ ḟaccaib cen anmuin.
42. Beiṙid- ṙium ona cenn na **muice** leiṙ
don ġobainn a coibche a inġine. Iṙ de ṙin
ata Sliab **muice** a Mumainn.

43. Do luid in ġilla ṗoime iaṙ ṙin i Connaċtaib, d'iaṙṙaid Cṙimaill mic Tṙénmóiṙ.

44. Aṁail ṙo buí ṙoṙ a ṙéd co cualaid
ġul na h-én mná. Luid ṙai co n-acca in
mnaí, ocuṙ ba déṙa ṙola cech ṙe ṙeċt, ocuṙ
ba ṙcéit ṙola in ṙeacht aile, co mba **deṙġ**
a bél.
45. Iṙat bél **deṙġ,** a ben, ol ṙé. Ata
deiṫbiṙ ocum, ol ṙi; m'oen **mac** do maṙbad
d'oen laeċ ṙoṙ-ġṙanda móṙ do ṗála cuccum.
Cia ainm do ṁic, ol ṙé. Ġlonda a ainm,
ol ṙi.
46. [Iṙ de ata Aṫ n-Ġlonda ocuṙ Tóċaṙ
n-Ġlonda ṙoṙ Maenmuiġ, ocuṙ iṙ ó'n bél

(that it) went through her, so (that he) left her
without life.
42. He brings then (the) head of the pig **with**
him **to** the smith, in (*as*) dower of his daughter.
**It is from** that is (called) **the** pig's mountain **in**
Munster.
43. The youth **went** before him (*forward*) **after
that** into Connacht, to seek Crimall, **son** of Treun-
**mór** (his father's brother).
44. So (he) was on his road till (he) heard (the)
cry of [the] one woman. He goes towards her till
**he saw** the woman, and (there) were **tears** of blood
**every** [with] time (*at one time*), and (there) **was a**

ṗin. Do ċuġ ṗe uṗċuṗ ⱱ'a ḟleiġ uiṗṗu, ⱱo ċuaiⱱ ṫṗiċi, ġuṗ ḟáġ ṗe í ġan anam.

42. Ḃeiṗ ṗe ceann na muice an tan ṗin leiṗ ⱱo'n ġoḃainn, maṗ ṗṗṗé ⱱ'a inġin. Iṡ ⱱé ṗin a tá Sliaḃ-na-muice a Mumain aṗ n-a ġaiṗm.

43. Do ċuaiⱱ an ġiolla ṗoiṁe iaṗ ṗin a ġ-Connaċt ⱱ'iaṗṗaiⱱ Ċṗimaill mic Ṫṗeun-ṁóiṗ, eaⱱon, ⱱeaṗḃṗátaiṗ a ataṗ.

44. Aṁail ⱱo ḃí ṗe aiṗ a ḟliġe ġo ġ-cualaiⱱ ṗe ġul aon-ṁná. Ṫṗuall ṗe uiṗṗu ġo ḃ-facaiⱱ ṗe an ḃean, aġuṗ ⱱo ḃí ⱱeoṗa ṗola ġaċ ṗe ṗeaċt, aġuṗ ⱱo ḃí ṗġeit ṗola ṗeaċt eile, ġo ṗaiḃ a ḃeul ⱱeaṗġ.

45. Iṡ ḃeul-ⱱeaṗġ a tá tu, a ḃean, aṗ ṗe. Tá eiġean oṗm, aṗ ṗí;—m'aon ṁac ⱱo ṁaṗ-ḃaⱱ le laoċ uṗ-ġṗánⱱa móṗ ⱱo ċáṗla teaċt ċuġam. Caⱱ é ainm ⱱo ṁic? aṗ ṗe. Ġlonⱱa a ainm, aṗ ṗí.

46. [Iṡ ⱱé a tá áṫ Ġlonⱱa aġuṗ Tóċaṗ Ġlonⱱa aṗ Maonṁáġ aṗ n-a nġaiṗm;

vomiting of blood the other time (i.e., *every second turn*), till her mouth was red.

45. Thou **art** red-mouthed, O woman, says he. **There** is **a** cause with me (for it), says she; my **one son to** be slain (i.e., *that my only son was slain*) by **a** very-large hideous warrior who happened (to **come**) towards **me**. What (was the) name of thy son? said he. Glonda (was) his name, said she.

46. [It **is from him are** (called) Glonda's ford and Glonda's causeway on Maonmhagh; and it is from that red mouth is (called) Ford of red-mouth from that (time) forth (*ever since*)]

ueiριʒι ριn a τa Áτh m-bel υeιριʒι ó ριn ι
Le].

47. Luιυ υιn Fιnυ ιn υeʒaιυ ιn Laích, ocuρ
ρeριαιτ comlonn ocuρ υο ρuιτ laιρ é. Iρ am-
Laιυ ιmορρυ buí ριn, ocuρ coρρ-bolʒ na ρéυ
aιʒι .ι. ρeοιυ Cumuιll. Iρ e υιn υο ρochaιρ
ann ριn .ι. Lιaτ Luacρa, ιρ é céυ ʒuιn Cumull
ι caτh Cnucha.

48. Téιυ ι Connaċτaιb ιaρ ριn, ocuρ ρaʒeιb
Cριmall ιn a ρenóιρ a n-υιτhρeιb caιlle anυ,
ocuρ υρem υο'n ρeιn-Féιnn maιlle ρριρ, ocuρ
ιρ ιαυ ριn υο ʒní ρelʒa υο.

49. Tócbaιυ ιn coρρ-bolʒ υιn υο ocuρ
aτρeτ a ρcéla ó τúρ co υeιρe, ocuρ amaιl
ρο maρb ρeρ na ρéυ.

50. Ceιlebρaιυ Fιnn υο Cριmall, ocuρ Luιυ
ροιme υ'ροʒlaιm éιcρι co Fιnnécep ρο boí ρορ
boιnn. Nιρ lam umορρο beιτh a n-Éριnn
cena no co n-υechaιυ ρe ριlιυeċτ, aρ eaʒla
mac Uιρʒιunn ocuρ mac Mορna.

47. Fionn then went in (the) wake of the warrior, and they give combat, and he fell by him (Fionn). It is thus, moreover, was (he) [that], (*this is the way he was*), and (having) a round-bag of jewels with him, i.e. (the bag of) Cumhall's jewels. [It is he] (the) person who was killed there, i.e., Liath Luachra; it is he first wounded Cumhall in (the) battle of Cnucha.

48. (Fionn) goes into Connacht after that, and finds Crimall (in his) old man in a hermitage of a wood there, and a company of the old Fiann along with him, and it is they who used to make chases (*go a hunting*) for him.

agus is ó'n m-beul veaṗs ṗin a tá aċ-an-
ḃeil-ḃeiṗs ó ṗin a leiṫ.]

47. Cuaiḋ Fionn a n-oiaiġ an laoiċ ann
ṗin, agus ḃeiṗṗo cómlann, agus vo ċuit ṗe le
Fionn. Is amlaiḋ ṗin, umoṗṗo, vo ḃí ṗeiṗean,
agus coṗṗ-ḃolg na ṗeov aige, eaḋon, ṗeoiv
Cúṁaill. Is ṗe ṗóṗ vo tṗaṗgṗaḋ ann ṗin, an
té ġoin Cúṁall ais v-túṗ a g-caṫ Ċnuċa
.i. Liaṫ Luaċṗa.

48. Téiḋ Fionn a g-Connaċt iaṗ ṗin, agus
ġeiḃ ṗe Cṗimall 'na ṗeanóiṗ a n-víṫṗeaḃ
coille ann, agus vṗeam ve'n t-ṗean-Féinn
a maille leis, agus is ṗiaḋ ṗin vo ġniḋeaḋ
ṗealga ḋó.

49. Tuġaiḋ ṗe an coṗṗ-ḃolg ḋó ann ṗin,
agus inniṗṗó ṗé a ṗceula ó ċúṗ go veiṗe,
agus amail vo maṗḃ ṗe ṗeaṗ na ṗeov.

50. Gaḃaṗ Fionn cead le Cṗimall, agus
cuaiḋ ṗoime v'ṗóġluim éigṗe go Finnéiġeaṗ
vo ḃí aiṗ an m-Ḃoinn. Níoṗ láṁ ṗe, umoṗṗo, a
ḃeiṫ a n-Éiṗinn ċeana a n-áit aiṗ ḃiṫ, no
go n-veaċaiḋ ṗe le ṗilíḋeaċt [v'ṗóġluim,] aiṗ
eagla mac Uiṗgṗinn agus mac Móṗna.

49. He gives the round-bag then to him, and
relates his stories (*news*) from beginning to end—
and thus (*how*) (he) killed the man of the jewels
(*him who had the jewels*).

50. Fionn takes leave of Crimall, and went
before him (*forward*) to learn literature with
Finneigeas, who was (dwelling) on (the) Boinn.
(He) dared not even be in Eire anywhere until he
went with (i.e., to learn the art of) poetry, for fear
(of the) sons of Uirgreann, and (the) sons
of Morna.

51. Secht m-bliaḋna do Finnécir for Boinn oc urnaiġe iach Linne Feic; air do buí a ṫairrngire do eo Feic do tomailt, ocur cen ní na ainfir itir iarum.

52. Fritḣ in m-bradan, ocur ro h-eribaḋ do Deimne umorro in bradan do ruine, ocur arbert an file rrir cen ní do'n bradan do tomailt. Do bert in ġilla do an bradán iar na ruine.

53. In ar tomlir ní do'n bradan, a ġilla, ol in file. Nítọ, ol in ġilla, aċt mo óiṙou do loircer, ocur do radur im beolu iartain. Cia h-ainm fil ort-ra, a ġilla, ol re. Deimne, ol in ġilla. Finn do ainm, ol ré, a ġilla, ocur ir duit tucaḋ in bradan dia tomailt, ocur ir tu in Find co fír.

54. Toimlid in ġilla in bradan iartain. Ir rin tra do rat in fir do Finn .i. an tan do berèḋ a ordain i n-a beolu, (ocur noċan

51. Seven years (had been passed) by Finn-eigeas on (the) Boinn, watching (for the) salmon of (the) pool of Feic; for it was in prophecy to him (the) salmon of Feic to eat, and without a thing in his ignorance at all (*that he should know everything*) then.

52. The salmon was found (*caught*) and (it) was assigned to Deimne moreover the salmon to bake (or *roast*), and the poet said to him without (*not*) a thing (*portion*) of the salmon to eat (*that he should eat none of it*). The youth brought to him the salmon after [its] cooking.

53. Didst thou eat a thing (*any part*) of the

51. Cuaiḋ seaċt m-bliaḋna tar Ḟinnéi-geas air an m-Boinn, ag urnuiġe air braḋán Linne-Féic: óir do ḃí se a d-táirngire dó braḋán Féic do ċomailt, agus gan niḋ air biṫ a ḃeiṫ 'na ainḃrior air ar rin.

52. Fríṫ an braḋán, agus do h-órduiġeaḋ do Ḋeimne umorro an braḋán d'ḟuineaḋ, agus duḃairt an file leir gan niḋ de'n ḃraḋán do ċomailt. Tug an giolla an braḋán dó iar n-a ḟuineaḋ.

53. Ar ċomlair niḋ de'n ḃraḋán, a giolla? ar an file. Níor ċomlar, ar an giolla, aċt do loirgear m'órdóg, agus do ċuirear am' ḃeul iar rin í. Ca h-ainm a tá ort-ra, a giolla? ar re. Deimne, ar an giolla. Fionn d'ainm, ar re, a giolla, agus ir duit-re tugaḋ an braḋán d'a ċomailt, agus ir tura an Fionn go fíor.

54. Comlar an giolla an braḋán iar rin. Ir re rin, trá, do rad an fior d'Ḟionn, eaḋon an tan do ḃeireaḋ re a órdóg ann a

salmon, O youth? says the poet. No—says the youth; but my thumb I burned, and I put (it) in my mouth after that. What name is on thee, O youth? says he. Deimne, says the youth. Fionn (*fair*) (is) thy name, says he, O youth, and it is to thee (it) was given (*appointed*) (in prophecy) the salmon to eat (and not to me), and it is thou (who art) the Fionn truly.

54. The youth eats the salmon afterwards. It is that, by-the-way, that brought the knowledge to Fionn, i.e., the time he used to bear (*put*) his thumb in his mouth, (and not through *Teinm-laogha*) ; and the thing which was (*used to be*) in his

tria Teinmlaega), ocuṡ ro ḟaillṡiġea do
iaṡam in ní ro biḋ 'na ainṡir.

55. Ro ḟoġluim-ṡium in treiḋ de nemti-
ġiuṡ ḟilid .i. Teinm Laeġa ocuṡ Imuṡ ṡoṡ
Oṡna, ocuṡ Diceḋul dicennaib. Iṡ anḋ ṡin
do ṡoine Finn in láiġ ṡi oc ṡromaḋ a éicṡi:

 56. Cettemain cain ṡee! ṡo ṡaiṡ anḋ
  cucht!
Canait Luin laiḋ láin, dia m-beith Laiġaiġ
 ann.
Ġaiṡiḋ caí cṡuaiḋ dean, iṡ ḟocen ṡam ṡaiṡ
Ruidiġ ṡine ṡii: bṡuinne ceṡb caill cṡaib,

Ceaṡbuiḋ ṡam ṡuaill ṡṡuth, ṡaiġid ġṡaiġ
 luath linn,
Leataiḋ ṡolt ṡoḋa ṡṡaich, ṡoṡbṡuḋ canach
 ṡann ṡinn,
Fuabaiṡ diṡġell ṡceill ṡiġine, imṡuḋ ṡeiḋ
 ṡian ṡith ṡeana,
Cuiṡitheaṡ ṡal ṡuan, tuiġthiṡ blaṫ in bit.
  beṡaiḋ.

ignorance (*unknown to him previously*) afterwards
used to be manifested to him.

 55. He learned the three (things) which distinguish poets: i.e., *Teinm laogha*, and *Imus for
Osna*, and *Dicheadal do-cheannaibh*. It is then Fionn
made this lay testing his (knowledge of) literature.

 56. May! pleasing time! most excellent the
colour! Blackbirds sing a full lay; (O) if Laigh-
aigh could be there! the cuckoos cry strong (and)

beul (agus ní tré teinm-laoġa), agus do
ḟoillrigté dó iar rin an nid do bideaḋ 'na
aimḃsior.

55. D'ḟógluim reisean an trí a eisipideas-
luiġear ḟilid, eaḋon, an teinm-laoġa,
agus Imbor ais Orna, agus Dićeaḋal do ćeann-
naiḃ. Is ann rin do ṡinne Fionn an laoiḋ
ro ag deiṁniuġaḋ a éigre:

56. Ceuḋram caoin-ré! ró-ṡár an ḋat!
Canaid loin laoiḋ lán, dá m-beiḋeaḋ
laġaiġ ann!
Goisid cuaić go crua id dian, is ḟáil-
teać rár-ṡám;
Áille rine go ríor: ais imeal-ḋóisid
coillteaḋ craoḃ
Rićid rám-ṡuaill ais rrut; ionnruiġid
eić luaća linn:
Leaćnuiġid ṡolt ṡada ṡraoić, bláćuiġid
ceannḃán sann rionn.
Ionnruiġid uaćḃár obann: imrid reana
ag sić reid-ruan,
Cuisćeas an ráile a ruan: ṡoluiġid
bláća an bić. * * *

violent; it is welcome, noble summer! (the) brilliance of the weather always. [On] the margin
fringe of (the) woods (of) boughs (branching) the
summer swallows skim the stream; the swift
steeds approach (the) pool; (the) long hair of (the)
heath spreads (out); the fair weak bog-down
flourishes: sudden consternation attacks [the
signs;] the planets running in smooth course play;
(the) sea is put (to) rest, flowers cover the world.

# NOTES.

CONCERNING the ancient compilation called *Saltair Chaisil*, in which the original of this tract on the "Exploits on Fionn" is said to have been included, Professor O'Curry remarks: "Next after these (several lost books), . . . I would class the SALTAIR OF CASHEL, compiled by the learned and venerable Cormac Mac Cullinan, King of Munster and Archbishop of Cashel, who was killed in the year A.D. 903. At what time this book was lost we have no precise knowledge; but that it existed, though in a dilapidated state, in the year 1454, is evident from the fact that there is in the Bodleian Library in Oxford, a copy of such portions of it as could be deciphered at that time, made by *Seáan*, or Shane O'Clery, for Mac Richard Butler. From the contents of this copy, and from the frequent references to the original, for history and genealogies, found in the Books of Ballymote, Lecan, and others, it must have been a historical and genealogical compilation of large size and great diversity."—(Lectures MS. Materials p. 19.) The same author (pp. 11 and 12), shows the origin of the word "Saltair" as applied to such compilations as the "Saltair of Teamhair," by King Cormac, son of Art, and the "Saltair of Caiseal" (its companion volume) by King Cormac, son of Cuillionan. He quotes, translating from Keating, this passage: " And it is because of its having been written in poetic metre that the chief book which was in the custody of the Ollamh of the King of Erinn was called the 'Saltair of Temair;' and the chronicle of holy Cormac Mac Cullinan, 'Saltair of Caiseal;' and the chronicle of Aengus Ceile Dé [or the 'Culdee'] 'Saltair-na-Rann' [that is, 'Saltair of the Poems or Verses']; because a *Salm* (Psalm) and a Poem are the same, and therefore a *Salterium* and a *Duanaire* [book of poems] are the same." In the present case and others, however, plain prose seems to have been admitted. The name, then, is taken from *the Psalter*. In his introduction to "Leabhar na g-Ceart," Dr. O'Donovan remarks of the Saltair of Caiseal, so frequently cited in that work, and in which that compilation is said to have been the book in which St. Benean entered the traditions respecting the rights and tributes of the kings of Munster: "These accounts (in Book of Rights, Colgan, Keating, Conall Mac Eochagain) look rather conflicting, but the probability is that they are all **true**, *i.e.*, that St. Benean commenced the Psalter; that Cormac (son of Cuillionan) continued it down to his own time . . . **and** that King Brian had a further continuation framed **to his** time." The reader will do well to consult O'Curry's "Lectures" especially on the subject of the poetical productions ascribed to Fionn, Oisin, Caoilte, &c.

In an able and interesting series of articles on "The Ossianic Tales," by Rev. J. J. O'Carroll, S.J., in the *Irish Ecclesiastical Record*, the rev. author, in No. 11 (December, 1880), has carefully and judiciously analysed this fragment—the Exploits of Fionn—in a critical disquisition, from which **we** regret space does not permit extracting more than the following few points. He says: "This work appears to have been selected on account of the archaic nature of its Irish. It is extremely short, a fragment certainly, perhaps only **an** introduction. Much will not be expected from it in the **way** of great literary development. In it, however, **as in other** Irish prose tales, passages of verse are carefully **introduced** from time to time. They are not brought **in as the** production of the author of the prose; such **a thing** would have been a strange irregularity indeed in masters of the art of composition, the **art** of producing a homogeneous whole from various **parts**. They come as illustrations of what is mentioned **in the** prose, and are not so long as to be possibly mistaken **for** anything more. They cannot obscure the clear progress **of** the tale. It so happens that the verses, in the middle of one line of which the archaic tract on Fionn's boyish exploits breaks off abruptly, are those selected by Mr. Standish O'Grady the historian to praise most specially in his essay on Irish 'Early Bardic Literature.' He there calls them a ' poem by Fionn upon the spring-time, made, as the old unknown historian says, to prove his poetic powers—a poem whose antique language relegates it to a period long prior to the tales of *Leabhar na h-Uidhre*, one which, if we were to meet side by side with the *Ode to Night*, by Alcman in the Greek anthology, **we** would not be surprised.' . . . We may, if we will, suppose that after this the tract grew more interesting, and that the prose that remains is only a quiet introduction to grander passages. Unfortunately, in the now remaining fragment there is little literary merit, beyond the unquestionably picturesque and pathetic view presented by Fionn's being brought up in the woods away from the haunts of men, to save his life from his father's enemies, and by the visit of his mother, when he was six years old, to the forest **huntresses**, who were his nurses. The mother, indeed, **is here** described **in a way** that seems to show not **only insight into human nature, but** graphic power in the **author. . . . And we may well** be right in thinking that **the author who described so** touchingly the visit of the **mother who travelled from solitude** to solitude that she **might be able to set eyes for a few hours on** her child ; the **author who thought of making the mother** find the boy **asleep in the rude hut of his forest home,** and who represents **her as unwilling to disturb his slumber,** and cradling **him on her bosom, the author who makes** her pour forth **her feelings in a lullaby to the** unconscious child, **was one too rich in real sentiment to be** showily or gaudily **extravagant in speech ; was a man who would** scorn to make **grand passages out of the direct recital of** Fionn's boyish **feats.** With the fine description of the mother's visit **we believe we may venture to do a very** bold thing. We are **going to set beside it a parallel passage** from one of the **greatest poets that ever lived, and to compare or rather to contrast the two.** Spenser, **as well as our anonymous ancient Irish writer, puts before us a child of extraordinary strength and prowess, brought up in the woods, and visited one day by its mother. . . . For wonderful exploits we must admit that little Satyrane** beats young **Fionn hollow. For touching** beauty in **the** mother's visit, **we must look to** the work of our unknown Irish artist, not **to that of the** most justly world famous Edmond Spenser. **. . . In our Irish tale Fionn's mother** is one that would have been recognized **by Solomon. . . . All this is no mere outburst of sudden feeling, no natural** outcome of necessary circumstances ; **it is a scene most** delicately chosen, most carefully contrived ; **it is. in truth, one** of the intelligible cases of Selection of the Fittest."

The legend of the "Salmon of Knowledge" (Eo feasa) **is very ancient and** curious, and is to be met with in a variety of forms. **It is not** unfamiliar to our modern story-tellers who furnish many **versions** of it, as well as of Fionn's gift **of knowledge ; how he came by it, and the method he used to** avail himself **of it** at need. Such are the story of "**Canuran Caoch," and** many others, in popular books. Professor O'Curry **writes :** "The history of Finn Mac

Cumhaill's 'Thumb of knowledge,' as related in the ancient tales, is very a wild one, indeed ; but it is so often alluded to that I may as well state it here, (Lectures, p. 396). It is shortly this: Upon a certain occasion this gallant warrior was hunting near *Sliabh na m-ban* in the present county of Tipperary ; he was standing at a spring-well, when a strange woman came suddenly upon him, filled a silver tankard at the spring, and immediately afterwards walked away with it. Finn followed her, unperceived, until she came to the side of the hill, where a concealed door opened suddenly, and she walked in. Finn attempted to follow her farther, but the door was shut so quickly that he was only able to place his hand on the door-post with the thumb inside. It was with great difficulty he was able to extricate the thumb ; and having done so he immediately thrust it, bruised as it was, into his mouth to ease the pain. No sooner had he done so than he found himself possessed of the gift of foreseeing future events. This gift, however, was not, we are told, always present, but only when he bruised or chewed the thumb between his teeth. Such is the veracious origin, handed down to us by the tradition of the poets of Finn Mac Cumhaill's wonderful gift of prophecy!"

This is one version of the origin of Fionn's knowledge ; the legend of Fionn and Canuran is another; the tract now under consideration supplies a third, and the most ancient—and there are others, including a legend in which Cormac appears as a party. Perhaps if the remainder of this piece, which we have only as a fragment, had been preserved to us, we might know as much as Fionn himself. The thirst after knowledge, and that too of a kind not usually granted to man, seems to have troubled many mortals, male and female, since Eve first stole the apple. Fionn in touching the roasted salmon humbly followed her example, and burned his fingers. What the precise knowledge was he obtained by this act we cannot now know, but he seems often to have been able to utilise it in getting his friends out of scrapes. See among others the " Legend of the Quicken-tree Palace," translated by Dr. Joyce (Old Celtic Romances). Miss Brooke says in a note on the verse, in the poem of "The Chase," "What does he do, but daily dine upon his mangled thumb." "This strange passage is explained by some lines in the poem of *Dubh mac Dithribh*, where Fionn is reproached with deriving all his courage from his foreknowledge of events, and chewing his thumb for prophetic information. The reader will easily perceive the source of this ridiculous mistake of the wonder-loving multitude; a habit taken up when deep in thought, was construed into divination; and we may conclude how great that wisdom, and that heroism, must have been, which was supposed no other way to be accounted for than by gifting the possessor with inspiration. In the romance of *Feis Tighe Chonain*, among other curious particulars, Fionn is said to have derived a portion of his knowledge from the waters of magical fountain, in the possession of the Tuatha De Danan; a single draught of which was sold for three hundred ounces of gold—."

The youthful exploits of Fionn were of a nature calculated to fit him for membership of the Fiann, and perhaps are, after all, only an imaginative account of some adventures he actually did meet with, during his time of probation. Our histories give detailed accounts of the training required to qualify for admission into that famous body. Dr. Keating, in particular, is very circumstantial; to O'Mahony's translation of his work we refer the reader. With respect to the life in tents, *fiann-bhotha*, and the hunting expeditions, which formed so notable a part of his education and of his occupation afterwards, the "Dissertations" of Dr. Chas. O'Conor of Balenagar, may be consulted. He says (p. 57), "The chase was a sort of military school. . . . These hunting-matches continued several days. . . . At nights they encamped in the woods, and reposed in booths, covered with the skins of the animals they hunted down. In the void spaces of the forests they exercised themselves in the military dances, wherein, generally, the most expert regulated the evolutions." And, p. 111. "It" (the practice of the chase), "gave them great muscular strength, great agility, and firmness against the severity of the most rigorous seasons; it besides taught them vigilance, skill in archery, and great patience under long abstinence from food. They came out of the forest expert soldiers, and no nation could excel them in rapid marches, quick retreats, and sudden sallies. By these means it was that they so often baffled the armies of South Britain and the Roman legions united." See also Keating for an account of the manner of living of the Fiann and a description of their cooking-places, or "Fulachta Feinne." We may learn, likewise, from allusions in the text, (such as at pars. 31 and 48) how necessary hunting was even for subsistence in those days, so that it became a duty for the younger folk to hunt the game for those who were old or incapacitated for pursuing the chase.

The poem by Fionn, with which this piece concludes, has been often quoted in Dr. O'Donovan's English version; it is very obscure, and but a mere fragment. A very pleasing metrical version of it has been made by Mr. A. P. Graves in his "Irish Songs and Ballads," together with several other ancient pieces. Mr. Standish O'Grady says of this poem and its author, in his "History of Ireland" (vol. i., p. 32): "The Ossianic cycle rolls on, bringing before us the last generation of the Fianna. There is their captain and ruler Fionn the son of Cool. His hair is white and lustrous, but not with age. It falls down over his wide shoulders. His countenance expresses more than the warrior and the hunter. For the delight of the noble-faced son of Cool was to sleep by the cataract of Assaroe, to hear the scream of the sea-gulls over Eyerus, to listen to the blackbird of Derry Carn, and to see ships tossing in the brine. He was nursed by the Shee of Slieve Blahma, and tutored by poets in the forests of the Galtees, where he, too, practised the art of the bards, not without success." "Over Fionn floats the banner of the Fianna, the likeness of the rising sun half seen above the horizon," *i.e.*, *Galgréine*, or the "Sunburst." In this portion of Mr. O'Grady's graphic work it seems like an anachronism to introduce the Fianna so long before the period when, according to all the authority we have, they flourished; but it is still stranger to bring Fionn, Caoilte, Oscar, Conan, Diarmuid, and Oisin himself, present with the "blessed Shee," consoling, in his mysterious anguish, the great Cuchullainn, who lived some three centuries before the earthly career of these worthies began, and before they-could have been placed among the "immortals."

The honour of being the earliest compositions in any vernacular tongue has been often claimed for certain Teutonic and Scandinavian poems. Our ancient literature dates earlier than any of these, and some of the Irish poems can be traced back to the days of paganism, and shown to be contemporaneous even with classical writings; yet, be it ancient or modern, the literature of Ireland is ruled out of court in an inquiry into the early works of European nations, even by such a writer as Mr. Longfellow. And hear Mr. O'Grady again (vol. ii., pp. 38 and 39), on the "Early Bardic Literature of Ireland:" "How then has the native literature of Ireland been treated by the representatives of English scholarship and literary culture? Mr. Carlyle is the first man of letters of the day, his the highest name as a critic upon, and historian of, the past life of Europe. Let us hear him upon this subject, admittedly of European importance ('Miscellaneous Essays,' vol. iii., p. 136): 'Not only as the oldest tradition of modern Europe does it—the Nibelungen—possess a high antiquarian interest, but farther, and even in the shape we now see it under, unless the epics of the son of Fingal had some sort of authenticity, it is our *oldest* poem also.' Poor Ireland, *with her hundred ancient epics*, standing at the door of the temple of fame, or, indeed, quite behind the vestibule out of the way! To see the Swabian enter in, crowned, to a flourish of somewhat barbarous music, was indeed bad enough—but Mr. MacPherson! They manage these things better in France, *vide passim*, La *Revue Celtique*."

The popular legends concerning Fionn, his son Oisín, and the Fiann in general, are innumerable, but are becoming every day more vulgarized, being so far removed from the ancient simplicity of style and grace of language, and so much interlarded with vulgar inventions as to be now almost valueless since the old art of story-telling, once so important, has all but died out with its professors. See legends printed in the *Irish Penny Magazine*, *Dublin Penny Journal*, *Irish Penny Journal*, &c., some of which, those by Edward Walsh in particular, will repay perusal. Several vulgar versions of the exploits of Fionn, originally based, most likely, on this ancient tract, are given in these volumes, and may be heard in the south and west.

TITLE. *Mac-ghniomhartha* is one of these compound terms which would have delighted Keating. *Mac*, a son, is often used for a boy or youth in old writings, as *inghean*, a daughter, is for a girl or woman (see par. 18). *Gniomhartha*, or *gníomha*, is the plural of *gníomh*, an act, exploit, or action; thus the whole signifies the youthful or boyish exploits of Fionn. We have preferred the present Irish spelling Fionn to Finn. The "n" in the former retains its broad sound, whereas in the latter, following "i," it would be slender, and thus would be likely to be sounded contrary to the pronunciation of Irish speakers. In the south, in particular, where the name is generally pronounced *Fiune*, the broad sound is very noticeable. Finn would be more usually sounded very nearly *Fing*. Besides, *Finn* is now more generally used as the genitive form. The geniive singular of proper names of individuals and places is generally aspirated, as we have it here in *gníomhartha Fhinn*, the deeds of Fionn. Some object to this branch of the system of mutation as having a tendency to weaken the language, and in the case of such a letter as *f* (which when aspirated becomes entirely silent) it might be dispensed with, and perhaps in others, for the sake of euphony. But it has its use, there are clear rules to guide it, and several nice distinctions can be pointed out by its aid. In family names, for instance, as explained by Dr. O'Donovan in his "Grammar," and from him by the present writer in the "Second Irish Book," the initial is not aspirated after *ua* or *mac*, except when these prefixes to Gaelic patronymics are themselves in the genitive case after another noun, or when they signify the son or descendant of a particular individual, without being the family name or surname of the person spoken of. Also in names of places compounded of two or more words, where the second portion is a proper name of an individual (as so often happens), the initial is never aspirated, as in *Cill-Peadair*, &c. But in such a phrase as *Teach Mhichil*, Michael's house, *Muillean Phádraic*, Patrick's mill; where it refers not to the name of a place but to the possessions, actions, or attributes of an individual, aspiration takes place. For the sake of these distinctions between names of individuals and of families, between individual possessions and topographical terms, the system of aspiration ought in this instance to be strictly followed out and the rules on the subject adhered to. Besides, in these cases it is common to the other Celtic tongues, and some carry it much farther than we do. Thus the Scottish Gael write and pronounce Mac Mhuirich and Mac Dhomhnaill with the ancestral name aspirated in its initial, which has caused the MacDonnells of Antrim to be sometimes called MacConnell. The Scotch, also, often use it in the second component part of names of places, contrary to the Irish system: so do the Welsh, as in *Llanbedr*, *Llanfair*, &c., where their system of mutation is followed. This is carrying it too far, and the distinctions which are so useful in Irish are lost sight of. In the present case *Mac Cumhaill* would simply mean Mac Cooll as a family name; but *Mac Chumhaill* is the son of (the individual) Cumhall, and at once indicates who is meant. (See note on *Fághail craoibhe Chormaic*.) In Fionn's time, of course, and for many ages afterwards, there were no surnames in Ireland, so the

system which developed later on does not apply in **its full
extent**. *Ann so síos*, here below. *Síos* signifies **down
or below** n reference to motion ; *shíos*, when **rest is
implied** ; but *ann so síos* is considered to mean not exactly down here *on this spot*, but immediately below,
or following, so *s* **is** not aspirated. Most of our ancient
pieces have **the** title stated in this way, **often** added
at **a** later date and by **a** different hand on the manuscript,
**or by the copyist, as most** probably in the present
**case**. At the end the first word was generally repeated
(**see last paragraph of Fleadh Duin** na ngeadh and **Cath
Muighe Rath, &c.**), **which was** very necessary, as the pieces
**follow each other in the old** books without any interval.
**As this tract is imperfect, the** repetition cannot be perceived, but the title is given as we have it. So close are
the **"selections" placed together in** our old books that
**often the title of most important** pieces is merely inserted
**afterwards** between the **lines**. *Sliocht*, posterity, race, **is
here used for an** extract **or** portion taken from, and is so
**employed** in cases like the present. Compare *Atlantis*, vol.
i., p. 370 ; and *Leabhar na h-Uidhre*, f. 43. See also title
of **Crowe's** edition of *Sceula na h-Eiseirghe*. *Saltair Chaisil*.
See first note above, preface, and Dr. O'Donovan's letter.

PARAGRAPH 1*a*. *Do rála*, happened, was waged, took
place. *Ladhaim .i. cuirim*, I put, send, wage (O'D. Supp.) ;
a contention, **a conflict** (p. 683). See note **on v.** 10 "Tir
na n-óg." *Do cuireadh* (passive) or *do thairluigh* (active)
is an equivalent for *rála*.

*b* [*Fiannuigheacht*][*Chieftainship of the Fiann*, **i. e., the**
leadership of the Irish militia.—O'D. From the **fact of
this** contention **about the** leadership of **the Fiann, and
from other portions** of this tract, particularly his being
**trained to take rank in** that body, we can learn that Fionn
**was not the founder of** the famous Praetorian **guards of
Eire, however he** may have developed or **reconstituted**
that renowned "militia;" and it cannot be very **clearly
shown when or** by whom they **were** established. **One
thing is certain, that,** as a corps, **they did not survive the
fatal field of Gabhra.** They were most probably **at first
the household troops of** the Airdrigh, and bore **in fight
the** *Gal-grèine* **or** sunburst, which afterwards was in **a
sense** regarded as **their** peculiar cognisance, rather than as
**the National Banner.** A valuable account of Cumhall,
**Fionn's father, is** given by Professor O'Curry, in his Introduction to *Cath Muighe Léana* ; see p. x, where it is

stated that Cumhall was captain of the Fiann under Conn Céadchathach. The opening portion of that work alludes to the origin of the battle of Cnucha, the causes of which are related in the introduction.

c *Cumhall*. The best account of this military leader will be found in the "Battle of Cnucha," preserved in the Book of Lismore.—O'D. Although here defeated, Cumhall the "victorious" was one of the bravest warriors of ancient Eire. His *dún* was at Rath Cumhaill (Rathcoole), in the present county of Dublin, and but a few miles from the fatal field of Cnucha. *Imfich*, a contention (see par. 5, *fich*). *fichim*, I fight (now obsolete), a word which is clearly cognate with the English word *fight*, if, indeed, it be not the root of the latter. The origin of many English words is Celtic, although in some cases a false etymology has long passed current for them. The English word "differ" is probably from the Latin, yet the Irish *dithbhir* closely resembles both, and being found in some of our oldest writings, is not likely to have been borrowed ; so our people to this day when they say, in speaking English, "it makes no *differ*," really use, not a corruption of the English word, but the old native term. *Deabhtha*, gen. of *deabhadh* or *deabhaidh*, a dispute, a lawsuit, now obsolete, (O'D. Supp.) is probably connected with this word, as also *deithbhir*, cause, need, occasion (see par. 45) and *deifir*, haste, instead of which latter *deithneas* is very generally heard in the South. See O'Don. Supp. to Dicty. *in voce deithbhireas*, lawfulness, legality, necessity, cause ; and *deithbhir*, necessary, with many examples.

d *Luaighni*, a famous military sept in Meath, descended from Luaighni, one of the brothers of Conn *Céadchathach*. *Ogygia*, Part III., c. 57.—O'D.

e *Cuil Contuinn*, a territory situated on the borders of the present counties of Meath and Cavan.—O'D.

f. *Ui Tairsigh*, see *letter*, p. 72.

2a. *Torba*, see *letter*, *id*.

b. *Earnanaibh*. Diarmuid and Grainne (Oss. Soc., p. 122, vol. 3) has this note—" Teamhair Luachra was also called Teamhair Earann, being the royal residence of the country of the Earna, or the descendants of Oillioll Earann, commonly called in English the Ernaans of Munster. It was situated in the district of Sliabh Luachra. Though Teamhair Luachra no longer exists, its site is marked by Beul atha na Teamhrach, a ford on a small stream near Castleisland in the county of Kerry."

*c. Muireann, Muirne*, see *letter*, also note, p. 58.

*d. Cnucha.* Conall Maceochagain states in his translation of the Annals of Cluanmacnois, A.D. 726, that this is the place called Castleknock [near the river Liffey, county of Dublin].—O'D. Here there is a tumulus or "barrow," which probably commemorates this battle.

3. *Ag tabhairt*, giving, i.e., waging or fighting. *A bh-farradh*, in company with, on the side of, a compound preposition, which governs the genitive, *farradh* being a noun. *'Na bh-farradh*, in their company, of their party. "Is truagh gan oidhir 'na bh-farradh"—*Davis' Lament for the Milesians* (quotation from Mac Firbis). *N-aill*, or *eile*, other, or *oile* another. Compare Welsh *ail*, second; in Swedish, also, the second is called the other. *Múnchaomh*, fair-necked. Compare ceanndána, ceannmhór, múnramhar, lámhfada, &c.

4*a. Iaram*: iaramh (see par. 28), an expletive equivalent to indeed, then, just, also, &c., in English. *Idir, dan*, and *tra* are also used in this way. See paragraphs 5, 31, 41, and 51. **Iaramh** is probably the word we often see Anglicised "eroo" and "iero" in plays and novels, put into the mouth of the peasantry, like the vulgar forms of *ar eadh? an eadh? maiseadh*, &c. *Do berar, bheirthear*, is given, is fought, past, *tugadh*. *Do* goes before such verbs as *bheir, gheibh*, &c., even in the present tense, so the initial is always aspirated. See *Faghail craoibhe* par. 2, &c. *Gonus, gonas*, historical form of the present tense of *goin*, wound. *Co ros mill*, i.e. *go ro mhill se*, till he destroyed. *A leth-rosc*, i.e., *a leath-shúil*, rosg not being now used except sometimes in poetry. One of a pair is expressed by *leath*, half; as it were that the two were required to form one perfect member; so a leath-shúil means one of his eyes.

*b Goll* is glossed *Caoch*, and means one-eyed, the same as the Latin *Luscus*.—O'D.

*c. O shin a leith*, from that time out, from that on (one) side, or apart.

5*a. Gonas.* See note 4 *a. Fear coimheuda*, the keeper, man of keeping; a compound word. Fear coimheuda corrbhoilg a sheod féin is nominative case to gonas, Cumhall being accusative after that verb, Dan, then, *expletive*.

*b Corr-bholg*, i. e., a round bag, *sed* [*seod*] means a jewel or any article of value.—O'D.

*c. Foidb*, spoils, arms, *spolia* taken in fight. Goll took the head, weapons and ornaments of Cumhall as a trophy, according to custom. *Conid:* go **n-it,** go n-id (old form of is) : that it is ; i.e., gur ab é sin, gur dé sin, so it is from that (followed), &c. *Cet*, chan, sang ; can and cet are the same ; as we see *céad*, Irish ; *cant*, Welsh ; and *cenum*, Latin : *cheud*, Irish ; **cyntaf**, Welsh. Compare in par. 12 *gaed*, for *goin*.

6*a*. *Co m-blaid*, i. e., go m-bládh, with renown, famous. Compare *go leor*, plentiful : go is sometimes prefixed to nouns, but **very** rarely, in the same way as it is put before adjectives **to form** adverbs. In these paragraphs many instances like the present occur, such as *co ngail*, &c. In Italian something similar occurs as *con amore ;* as it were *go ngrádh*, for *go grádhach*, or *go grádhmhar*, and in English this construction is not unknown. Sometimes in Irish too a noun or adjective with *go* prefixed retains its meaning without changing to an adverb. Compare *go h-Ailioch Neid go n-deagh-nós :* To Aileach Neid, of good **custom**. Keating, p. 78, Joyce's edition.

*b Fionnmhagh*, otherwise *Maghfionn*, a plain in the barony **of** Athlone, county of Roscommon, at this period possessed **by the** Firbolg, of whom the Clanna-Morna were a sept.—O'D.

7. *Nocha.* See *nochan*, par. **54** ; and *nitho*, 53. **Cha**, found in Ulster and Scotland as a negative, is an abbreviation of *nocha*, now obsolete. Do rochair, at rochair, fell, was killed. See rochair, fell, defective verb, in O'Donovan's Supplement. The *do* here is, perhaps, a mere prefix, like *at* prefixed to the same word elsewhere (see O'Don. Gram. p. 255) ; or it may be the sign of the passive past tense ; but if so, the sense is complete without it. See do aithrioghadh, was deposed, O'D. Gram. p. 255.

9. *Fear Fáil*, i. e., *fear inse Fáil*, [of the] men of Inisfail. (See Keating, chap. 1.) *Luaighne*, see notes pp. 55 and 62.

**10.** *Co m-buaidh* (see note **on** par. 6) is equivalent to *na* **m-buaidh**, of the victories ; Cumhall the victorious, **Cumhall of the hosts, as** he is called. **See letter, p.** 70, and **note, also note,** pp. 55 and 64.

11*a. Co torchuir.* See note **par. 7.** Dhé, **from or of that** ; i. e., in consequence of **the** compact then made between Fionn and Goll.

*b Teamhair Luachra*, a place in Kerry, not far from Castleisland, in the district of Sliabh Luachra.—O'D. See 2*b*.

12. *Aodh budh ainm.* Compare with this idiom Niamh chinn-óir is se m' ainm, (*Tir na n-óg* p. 3) : Muadhan m' ainm (*Diarmuid agus Grainne*) : Cetura ainm (*Foras feasa*). See also par. 3—**Ainm** eile, &c. *Aine,* i.e. *brigh ·* compare "Luir-

each Phádraic," *Aine teineadh*, the force of fire. *Conruitea*. See *Conrethed*, they attain to; *Conroichet, roichenn*, he attains to, obtains, &c. (O'Don. Supp.): i.e. Goll appertained to him as a name.

13a *Ro accaibh*, old form for *d'fhág*, **past** tense: *f*, when aspirated, is often entirely omitted in old writings, of which there are many instances in Keating; **as** *anas* for *fanas*, &c.

*b Muireann.* This was very common as the proper name of a woman among the ancient Irish. It is explained in Cormac's Glossary, as meaning *mor-fhinn*, long-haired. O'D.

*c. Mnai*, for *mnaoi* (which now would be *dative* form), and *Muirne*, are old accusative forms of bean and Muireann, following the verb. A bheith aici, his being with her; or a bheith aige, to be with him. *Iardam, iartan, iarthan*, after (that) time, afterwards. *Coni*, See note par. 5. *De side*, de sin, from that. See note on interchange of *d* and *n*, par. 5.

*d Lamhraighe*, a people of Kerry.—O'D.

14a. *Luidh*. See note v. 10, *Tir na n-óg*. *Leo*, with them; we would now more idiomatically say *a maille leo*, or *a g-cóimhdeacht leo*, i.e., together with, or in company with them, in such instances as the present.

*b Sliabh Bladhma*, i. e., the mountain of Bladhma (*Ogygia* III., 16), now Slieve Bloom on the confines of the King's and Queen's Counties. It is sometimes called *Sliabh Smoil*. The summit of this mountain is called mullach eipeann [now Arderin], the summit of Erin, and from it, the O'Dunnes have taken the motto of mullach eipeann abú!—O'D.

*c. Foithribh, fásachaibh*, desert places. See *foitirbi*, i. e., *imaire no gort*, no *achadh*, O'Donovan Supp. *Itaide*, i. e., *a d-taide*, in concealment, in secrecy (see O'D), i. e., *a bh-folach. Deithbhir*, See note p. 55. *Tinnesnach, teannasnach*, strong-ribbed, a compound adjective. (Compare *taimhgheugach*, Imit.)

16. *Cidh trácht*, no *ciod trácht, lit.* what telling, i. e., what need of saying more about it: however: be that as it may, or such like phrase. *Atracht;* compare adracht or atracht, he arose; O'Don. Supp.: eirigh, arose, went. *Fogeib* or *gheibh*, found: *fo*, an old sign of the perfect tense. Fiann-bhoth, a hunting-booth. See note p. 50.

17. [*Codail, &c.*] The rest of this "Lullaby" is lost. Indeed it would appear from the shortness of the sentences, and the abrupt and flighty nature of the composition, that the whole

story has been very much condensed, and in some places mutilated.—O'D. This is very probably the case with many other of our ancient compositions—or rather they were never written down but in this shape, as it were to furnish the story-teller with a skeleton or notes of his tale, which he generally committed to memory, filling in the details at each recital.

18. *At bert, ber,* a form of *deir,* say, whence *dubhairt* i. e., do bheirt; at and do are prefixes. See note on par 7.

19a. *Praslacha (lacha,* a duck) seems to have been some kind of wild fowl; most authorities say a widgeon. See O'Daly's Jacobite Poetry (*Súil-chabharthadh Éireann,* p. 70, 1844, Edn., p. 58, 1866, Edn.) for *prasganach* or *frasgannach,* an adjective, signifying in flocks, gregarious (*fras* means a shower). There is a kind of black, long-legged water-fowl, called the *pas-lacha;* this must be the bird mentioned here.

*b* [*Futha, &c.*] *At them.* The original Irish is defective here. The words obviously omitted are supplied in brackets. In *Feis tighe Chonáin* [Ossianic Society, vol. 2.], p. 129, it is stated that Fionn in his first chase killed the *pras-lacha* widgeon?), and her clutch of twelve young birds.—O'D.

20a. *Aos,* folk, a class of people; aos céirde, artisans, artificers, folk of trade, or poetry, it being the great art; aos dána, poets, &c. The names here have not been identified. *Ite,* old form of *is*; is siad.

*b Crotta,* i. e., Crotta Cliach, now the [*Gailte*] Galty mountains [Sliabh g-Crot] in the south of the county of Tipperary.—O'D. The *c* here is eclipsed, the word being in the genitive plural; *g* is frequently put in modern writings where *c* was written in ancient times.

21. *Im,* a form of *am* for *an* the article, which spelling is still retained in Scottish-Gaelic before *b, p,* or *f,* as *am fear, am baile,* &c. *Buile,* a blister, a boil, *bolgach*: now generally used for the small-pox. *Carrach,* a scald head, mangy, bald; gearb, a scab, the itch; gearbach, scabbed.—O'Reilly's Dicty.

22. *Fidh-Gaibhle,* now Feegile, in the parish of Cloonsast, north of Portarlington, in the King's County. This was the name of a famous wood in Leinster, in which St. Berchan, the Irish prophet, erected his church of Cloonsast, the ruins of which still remain.—O'D.

24a. *Magh Life,* i. e., the plain of the Liffey; a very level plain in the county of Kildare, through which the River Liffey winds its course.—O'D.

*b. Co nos ;* old form for *go ro* or *gur*, which, however, would not now be used before this verb. We say *go bh-facaidh*, most irregular verbs, even in the past tense, taking the same forms of the particles as are used with the present. *Iomáin*, driving, tossing (the ball), or hurling, the **game** now called in Ireland and the Highlands *camánacht*, **golf,** or hurling ; **so** called from *camán*, the hooked or **crooked stick** with **which it is played.** It is very ancient, and not yet extinct, *Iomáin*, **driving,** is **now** generally written *tiomáin*.

25. *Bárach,* an old word for morning ; Welsh, *boreu*. The word is also obviously connected with the English *morrow*. *Iar n-a m-bárach,* on the morrow, now written *air an márach ;* athrughadh márach, after to-morrow ; i.e., **the** change of the morrow. *Atnagat*: *eirghid ; teidh- d,* **they** go, or come (against). See O'Reilly *athnaghaid,* v. they come.

26. *Fil,* the **old form is used instead** of the modern *ta,* or *atá : fuil* is **now a secondary form** employed after particles, an, go, &c. *Contuicti,* that is *tig,* comes, or *thiocfadh,* should come. *Cumachtachi,* i. e., from *cumhacht,* power, if ye are able : **ancient verb,** *cumcaim,* I can, I am able ; modern, *feudaim*. See *Cumachtu,* in O'Donovan's Supp. to Dictionary, *voce cumcaim,* and Grammar.

28. *In* for *an,* sometimes for *na, pl. In fairend :* i. e., an fhuirionn, the folk, the party, *Sceula na h-eiseirghe, Ind fairend,* p. 24, Crowe's Edition. *Macraidh,* collective noun, like *laochraidh, eachraidh,* &c. Compare cavalry, &c. *Imtheacht :* instead of *imtheacht,* to go, we would **now** say **teacht, to come,** in such a case. Imtheacht is made up of *im,* a particle obsolete in this sense, and teacht, coming ; i. e., the opposite to coming, *to go*. So *imthig,* from *im* and *tig* come, is a more correct form than imthigh, which latter spelling has doubtless arisen from a notion that the verb belonged of the class which end in *uigh* and *igh,* **which some** grammarians call the second conjugation : the inflections peculiar to this **class** of verbs are also, by usage, adopted with the verb **imthig ;** as *imtheochad,* &c. In the South, verbs ending in *igh* and *uigh* are pronounced with the *g* hard and unaspirated, and in the present case at any rate this is quite correct.

30. *Feacht* or *feachtas ann (fecht and),* **a** time (there **was)** in it ; once upon a time. This word often figures in story telling. *Imdiscir,* very nimble ; *im* prefix (intensitive in **this** case) and *discir,* "fierce, nimble, active."—O'R. *Ag*

(*agh*), a cow, a deer; both meanings are given, and probably in very remote times (long before Fionn) the same word was applied to both animals; in primitive languages one word often did duty for several objects. Thus *gabhar*, a goat, anciently meant also a *horse*, being possibly the same word with *capall*. See **Dr.** Joyce's Irish Names of Places, **first** series, fourth edition, p. 475. **Compare the** Latin *caper* and *caballus*.

31. *Sen-tuinn*, i.e., *Sean-duine*, an old **person, an old man;** an old woman. O'Reilly gives *seanduine*, **an old** man, *sean-tuinne*, **an** old woman, but there can **be no doubt** these **are the same** word and but mere **vagaries of** spelling. He also gives *duine*, "a man, either male or female, **a man, anyone."** In usage the term is now mostly restricted to the male, but like *homo* in Latin, it may include **the female.** When *fear*, equivalent to and cognate with *vir*, **is** employed, then, as in Latin, the man only can be meant. Thus "man," *an duine*, in the sense of all mankind includes of course men and women : so does *daoine*, **plural** of *duine*, and *sean-duine* here signifies an old woman. *Astud*, *fastughadh* (see note on omission of initial *f*, par. 13), to retain, to fasten. This is either itself the root, **or cognate** with the root of the English word *fasten*.

32. *Buain*, *bhuainn*, **now** written *uainn*, **from** us, but *bhuainn* is sometimes met with, and is in use in Scottish Gaelic. *Aicill*, watch; *for aicill* (obsolete) *air ti*, **on** design, spying (almost always with the intention of doing injury). This word gives the true meaning of Aicill, an old name of the hill of Skreen, **where** Cormac had his residence after he retired from government, and **where** *Leabhar Aicle* was composed. It signifies a watch **or observatory**; and we are told Teamhair (Tara) could be seen from Aicill, but Aicill could **not** be seen **from Teamhair.**

33a. *Loch Lein*, now the Lakes of Killarney.—O'D.

b. *Luachair*, i. e., Luachair Deaghaidh, a district in the now county of Kerry, containing [*Dhá chích Dhanan*] the two Pap mountains.—O'D. From **this name** we have the famous Sliabh Luachra, and the **name** *Ciarraighe Luachra*. O'Curry, in a note on Magh Léana, p. 24, says : "This was anciently called Luachair Dheadhaidh, i.e., Deadhaidh's rushy district. . . . This rushy territory extended from the bounds of the present county of Limerick **to** the Lakes of Killarney in Kerry, a considerable way into the present county of Cork."

c. *Beanntraighe*, a district in South Munster, believed to

have been co-extensive with the barony of Bantry in the county of Cork.—O'D.

34a. *As bert*, **see note** par. 18. *Dar lat* is a misreading or error in transcription for *dar liom*, methinks. *Amsaine*, amhsaine, military **service** (see O'D. supp.); from *amhas*, a mercenary soldier.

*b. Alba*, i. e., Scotland.—O'D.

35. *Ciarraighe*, **now Kerry.** The territory so called **extended in early times only** from Tralee to the Shannon. **Its more ancient** name would appear to have been Cairbrighe, or Corbraighe.—O'D. Perhaps the place here meant is really Cairbrighe, a district of West Cork, **which may formerly** have been more extensive than at present, **and have included the southern** half of what is now the county **Kerry ; i.e. from** the real *Ciarraighe* southwards. *Atnuig* or *adnaidh*, i.e., *fan*, stay.

36. *Luaighni*, see par. 9, **note** and letter, p. 72. *Nár, nachar*, that not, that may not ; *ut* for *at*, see note, par. 9. *Marbh*, kill, makes muirfead I will kill, in the future, thus avoiding the junction of *bh* with *f*, and being also distinguished from the inflections of *mair*, live ; so *mhuirfidh*, conditional, *mhuirfidhe*, conditional passive.

37. *Cuilleann* [*Ua g-Cuanach*]. This is the present name of Cullen, in the county of Tipperary, near the borders of **the county of Limerick.** It originally belonged to the territory of Coonagh, now a barony in the **north-east of the county of Limerick.**—O'D. In O'Donovan's "**Supplement to Dictionary**," we further find "*Cuilleann o g-Cuanach*, now **Cullen, a village originally in** the barony of Coonagh, **county of Limerick, on the border of the** parish of *Sulchoid*, in the county of Tipperary. *See* Annals of the Four Masters at the year 1579, and Book of Lismore, *fol.* 230, *a. a.*, where it is said to have taken its name from Cuilleann **the son** of Morna, who was killed here by Finn mac Cumhaill. Though this village was originally in the barony of Coonagh, as its name indicates, it is now considered as belonging to **the barony of** Clanwilliam, in the county of Tipperary." **The addition** " Ua g-Cuanach," or " of the O'Cuanachs," was added afterwards to distinguish this from other places of the same or similar name ; but this distinctive addition may have been **in use** long before the general adoption of surnames, and perhaps almost from Fionn's day, as tribes were even then distinguished by the name of an ancestor, though not in the same way as in more modern times. *Flaith-ghobha*, see Joyce's Grammar, p. 129, for an inte-

resting explanation of the expressive and useful idiom here employed, but which does not seem to have been as strictly adhered to in ancient times **as** it is now. *Adnaig,* see note, par. 35.

38. *Bér,* old form for *bhéarfad, future,* **I** will give; often used by Keating. *Cin co: gion go, gion gur (past),* although— **not.** Mr. S. H. O'Grady **says,** vol. 3, Oss. Soc., p. 136 :— " This expression is no longer used in the spoken language, and requires explanation. It has sometimes a negative meaning. . . . equivalent to **the present** *gidh nach.* . . . sometimes it is affirmative."

40. *Dia* **n-ab,** now *d'a n-ab,* or ***d'a r-ab.*** **The** *n* and *r* **here** being **merely** euphonic, it is **better to retain** *n* in the **present** tense (as in this case); *r* **being used in** a similar **position** when past time **is** indicated.

41. *Anam,* which **more** generally means a *soul,* is often **used,** even in **modern** works, to express *life* merely.

42a. *Coibhche,* see O'Don. Supp. to Dictionary, *in* **voce.** This marriage (if it can **be** called **such)** of Fionn with the daughter of the chief-smith, proves that matrimony **among** the pagan Gael **was just** what **it was** among the patriarchs. The father "**gave away**" his daughter (a relic of which still subsists), **but** instead of giving a dowry, **he received a** certain *pretium,* generally something he valued as much as the smith must have valued the head of the mysterious wild boar which had ravaged and devastated the country; **and** the destruction of which was the claim that enabled **an** unknown adventurer, as Deimne was at the time, to aspire to the daughter of the king of the smith's craft, which profession in ancient Ireland, as **in** early Rome, was held in high consideration, **and** had **its** legal rank **and** privileges clearly defined.

*b. Sliabh muice,* **i. e., the** pig's **mountain, now Sliev** Muck, situated between **the** town **of Tipperary and the** glen of Aherlow [*Eatharlach*].—O'D.

44. *Sét,* a road, a way; **an** ancient term for a small road, a path for one animal. **See** Book of Rights, Introduction, p. lvi. Probably from *sét* **or** *séd,* a heifer, now called *samhaisg.* From this **word** Cormac's Glossary derives *droichead,* **a** bridge, *direach,* direct or straight, and *séd,* i.e., the direct road—across the river. *Aon-mhná,* compare with this "ro chonnairc **an** t-aon óglach," in first paragraph of Faghail craoibhe. *Cech* **re** *fecht; gach le feacht,* every alternate time, i.e., by **turns.** See Idiom in Joyce's Grammar, p. 128. Feacht **is now** obsolete in

the spoken language, but is often met in very modern writings, not only in the present sense, but used at the opening of a story, as "feacht n-ann," which may be Englished "once upon a time." It is also used in composition, as *a n-aoinfheacht le*, at **one time** with, together with. *Le* is now generally used **in Ireland** for *re*, but the latter is retained exclusively in Scotland, and is employed occasionally in Ireland as **in the** Bible or writings of a solemn character. Both forms are **met with** side by side in very ancient writings, and, **most** probably, the difference is merely euphonic, the Irish, **like** the Spanish language, preferring the sound of *l*, as in *Caitilín*, *Catalina*, for *Catherina*.

45. *Isat*, **thou art.** See O'Donovan's Grammar, p. 161, for various old forms of **the verb** *is*. *Do mharbhadh*, i.e., *do bheith* **marbhtha**, active **used for** passive.

46. *Maonmhagh*, Moinmoy, a territory lying round Loch Reagh in the present county of Galway; but the situations of *Áth-Glonda*, i. e., the ford of Glonda, and of *Tochar-Glonda*, the causeway of Glonda, **are** now unknown by these names. *Áth Béildheirg*, i.e., the ford of Red-mouth, not identified unless it be Ballyderg.—O'D.

47. *Liath Luachra*. Here is identified **the** party who wounded Cumhall first, **one** of his own household; the ingrate falls by **the hand of** Fionn, son of Cumhall, who thus obtains his revenge quite unexpectedly. This same Laith seems to have wished to condone his crime (see par. **13 and** 14) by his attentive solicitude after young Fionn. **This** Liath bore the name Fionn. See also *Diarmuid* hnd *Grainne* **(Ossianic Soc.**, vol. **3,** p. 123-125), where the following **passage occurs:** "Conan the son of Fionn of Laithluachra is my name, and my father was at the slaying of thy father at the battle of Cnucha, and he perished himself for that act." So the well-known Conan Maol was son of the slayer of Fionn's father, from which and other causes arose the enmity between him and the leaders of **the Fiann. Liath** seems to have been **of** Clanna Morna.

48. *Connachtaibh*. The plural is often met for the singular; a g-Connachtaibh, a n-Ulltaibh, which probably **means among (or in the land** of) the Connacht or Ulster men. **For an opinion on this** point see Dr. Joyce's Keating notes, pp. **15—24.** Compare Regio Connachtorum, Provincia Muminensium, &c., in Dr. Reeves' Adamnan. See also *Dubhcharn a Laighnibh*, and *Almhuin Laighean* in Diarmuid and Grainne. *Fris, ris*, see note on par. 44.

49. *At fet*, he relates, obsolete. **See** note on par. 9, and O'Donovan's Grammar, p. 255.

50*a*. *Boinn*, i. e., the river Boyne, in Meath. [*Mac Mhorna*]. Here ends folio 119 of the original MS., and on the upper margin of folio 120, in the handwriting of the scribe, is the following observation:—"ᴀ ᴍᴜɪʀɪ, ɪꞅ ꝼᴀᴅᴀ co ᴛɪc emunn ón coɪnne." "O Mary [Virgin], it is long till Edmund comes from the meeting." This was Edmund Butler, for whom the MS. was transcribed.—O'D. See note, p. 53, on the aspiration of proper names in the genitive case.

*b*. *Filidhecht*. His taking to the study of literature and cultivating the art of poetry was, as we see, a protection to him against his numerous enemies, as a poet's life was sacred. Mr. O'Grady writes (vol. 2, p. 32): "A great English poet, himself a severe student, pronounced the early history of his own country to be a mere scuffling of kites and crows, as indeed are all wars which lack the sacred bard, and the sacred bard is absent where the kites and crows pick out his eyes. That the Irish kings and heroes should succeed one another, surrounded by a blaze of bardic light, in which both themselves and all those who were contemporaneous with them are seen clearly and distinctly, was natural in a country where in each little realm or sub-kingdom the ard-ollav was equal in dignity to the king, which is proved by the equivalence of their erics."

51*a*. *Urnuighe*, seeking, praying (for). The latter is the meaning now in use. *Eo, iach* gen., an old word for bradán, a salmon, also means a brooch, probably from the shape. See note on the "Salmon of knowledge," p. 48. Mr. O'Grady seems to consider this "Eo feasa" as being one of the manifestations of Fionntan mac Bochna, a mythical personage, who is said to have flourished in Eire before the Deluge, and survived to the advent of Christianity. His appearance as a fish bears a strong resemblance to the story of one of the multitudinous "incarnations" of Vishnu, and both are of course traces of the traditionary idea of the great Flood, preserved after the dispersion by all mankind for ages, together with the remembrance of the second father of the human race, the Xisuthrus of the Asiatics, the Fionntan of the Western Gael, the Noah of the Bible. The facts which had been handed down from their fathers, together with such portions of ancient revelation as they had preserved, however distorted by the inventions of different races, yet have sufficient of a resemblance to show their common source, and to reasonably account for the striking similarity of certain leading features of oriental religions with the teachings of the west. In the "History of Ireland," vol. 2, p. 90, we read: "**Of** this Titanic race, one individual survived, and **passed, as a** spiritual entity, into the serener assembly of the gods, his name Fionntan, the patron deity **of learned men.** He is identified with 'the salmon of all **knowledge**' who haunted Connla's sacred well, and **the Boyne, and the** depths of the ocean. In his divine character **he dwelt in** the hills above Loch Derg and in **the mountains of** Kerry, and devoted himself to poetry and **the** history of the nations of Erin. The author of **the** 'Battle of Magh Leana' refers to him as the source of **his** information concerning Conn." See p. 97, O'Curry's translation of "Cath Muighe Leana," where we find, "As was sung by the Salmon of all knowledge, the possessor of all intelligence, and the jewel manifestly rich in all history and in all truth, namely, Fionntan the prophetic, the truly acute, and the truly intelligent." See also Mr. O'Grady's twenty-sixth chapter of his first volume, where **he** writes of the great divine fountain, the source of the Sionna, and **the** "nuts" which formed the food of the "salmon" of **knowledge.** "Unseen by the Gaeil the fountain still springs, **feeding the great** stream of Fohla, and the hazels shed their **crimson fruit on** the mossy ground, **and** into the clear **water, and beneath** the ground it sends **forth rills** feeding the **great streams.** But at the time of the shedding of fruit, a salmon, **the** Eo feasa, appears in that garden in the clear well, and as each divine nut falls upon the surface he darts upwards and devours it. He is larger and more beautiful than the fishes of his tribe, glittering with crimson stars and bright hues; but for the rest of the year he roams the wide ocean and the **great** streams **of** Inis Fail." In one of these rambles, presum**ably,** he got to Linn Feic, and was "roasted" and eaten; **but of** course only vicariously, or in appearance, he being **immortal.** From his living in the sea through the Deluge, **and afterwards in the** great rivers, his surname is derived, Bochna signifying the **sea in a** local dialect used in Cork, Limerick, Clare, and Kerry, according to Mr. R. MacElligott (Trans. Gaelic Society, 1808), and which that author calls *Bérlagair na Saer*. *Bochna* is also met in some of the writings of the Munster poets of the last century, who employ many terms not to be found elsewhere. See O'Curry's introduction to Cath Mhuighe Léana, where the habits and haunts of this "salmon" are described, p. xxi. Fionntan is possibly a form of Fionn, or *Fionn-duine*, the "fair" man, as he is called : or Fionntan, fair land, mac Bochna, son of the sea, like Lear mac Allóid, in which name the sea is also the son of the land. We see here that the gift which the visionary salmon was to bestow was promised by ancient tradition to an individual whose name should be Fionn : Finneigeas, or "Wise Fionn," naturally expected it, and spent his seven years at Linn Feic "praying" for it, yet it was bestowed on another Fionn—son of Cumhall—who had not expected or known anything of it.

*b. Linn Feic*, the pool of Fec, a deep pool in the river Boyne, near "*Ferta fer fecc*," the ancient name of the village of Slane, on this river.—O'D. Linn Feic is a beautiful calm spot for a studious or contemplative man to pass his years by its shore ; and it was probably for that reason chosen by the famous St. Erc "of Slane" for his hermitage, a few centuries after Fionn's time. The ruins yet remain of a church occupying the site of St. Erc's cell. *Itir* is here an expletive like *iarum* (see note, par. 4) and is still frequently so used in Scottish Gaelic.

52. *Frith*, was found. Canon Bourke, in his Grammar, says this word is not yet obsolete, though very seldom heard.

53*a. Nito*, or natho, see note, par. 7, and O'Donovan's Grammar, p. 324.

*b.* [*Fionn d'ainm*] *Fionn is thy name, &c.* It appears that our hero had concealed from his master Finn-Eges that he had been known by the name of Fionn, after he had drowned the nine boys in Magh-Life. But the poet finding that he had first tasted of the salmon of *Linn Feic* without intending it, saw that the ancient prophecy was fulfilled in him, and that his real name must be Fionn. O'Flaherty states that our hero assisted his father-in-law, Cormac, son of Art, in compiling codes of laws ; and the Life of St. Columkille, compiled by Manus O'Donnell, states that he possessed the gift of prophecy, and foretold the birth and future greatness of St. Columkille.—O'D.

54. *Teinm Laogha*. For a curious account of this poetical incantation as given in Cormac's Glossary, the reader is referred to the "*Battle of Magh Rath*," printed for the Archæological Society, p. 46. It is said that St. Patrick abolished the *Teinm Laogha* and the *Imbas for Osna*, as being profane rites, and allowed the poets to use another called *Dichedal do chendaibh*, which was in itself not re-

pugnant to Christianity, as requiring no offering to false gods or demons.—O'D. Dr. O'Donovan further gives in his note at p. 46 of the Battle of Magh Rath the following explanation of the "prophetic" gifts of the Druids and Bards, which will be useful here : " In the times of paganism in Ireland every poet was supposed to possess the gift of prophecy, or rather a spirit capable of being rendered prophetic by a certain process. Whenever he was desired to deliver a prophecy regarding future events, or to ascertain the truth of past events, he threw himself into a rhapsody called *Imbas for osna*, or *Teinm Loeghdha*, during which the true images of these events were believed to have been portrayed before his mind. The following description of the *Imbas for osna*, as given in Cormac's Glossary, will show that it was a humbug not unlike the magnetic sleep of modern dreamers : '*Imbas for osna*.—The poet discovers through it whatever he likes or desires to reveal. This is the way it is done : the poet chews a piece of the flesh of a red pig, or of a dog or cat, and he brings it afterwards on a flag behind the door, and chants an incantation upon it, and offers it to idol gods ; and his idol gods are brought to him, but he finds them not on the morrow. And he pronounces incantations on his two palms ; and his idol gods are also brought to him, in order that his sleep may not be interrupted ; and he lays his two palms on his two cheeks, and thus falls asleep ; and he is watched in order that no one may disturb or interrupt him ; until everything about which he is engaged is revealed to him, which may be a minute, or two, or three, or as long as the ceremony requires: *et ideo* Imbas *dicitur*, i.e., *di bois ime*, i.e., his two palms upon him, i.e., one palm over and the other across on his cheeks. St. Patrick abolished this, and the *Teinm Leoghdha*, and he declared that whoever should practise them would enjoy neither heaven nor earth, because it was renouncing baptism. *Dichedul do chenduibh* is what he left as a substitute for it in the *Corus Cerda* [the Law of Poetry], and this is a proper substitute, for the latter requires no offering to demons.' These practices, about which so little has been said by Irish antiquaries, must look extraordinary to the philosophic inhabitants of the British Isles in the nineteenth century. But it is highly probable that some of the more visionary Germans will think them quite consonant with the nature of the human soul ; for in the year 1835, a book was published at Leipsig by A. Steinbeck, entitled 'Every Poet a

Prophet ; a Treatise on the *Essential* Connection between the Poetic Spirit and the Property of Magnetic Lucid Vision.'" These silly practices seem much of the stamp of some of the ceremonies connected with the Egyptian and Grecian oracles ; yet after all, perhaps, we may say "there is more in heaven and earth than is dreamed of in philosophy."

55. *Treid*, *treidhe*, now obsolete, three things. See preceding note.

56a. [*Ceud-Shamh*] *May-day*, ceccemaın, is glossed beLL- caıne by O'Clery. It signifies the beginning of summer.— O'D. *Lá Béaltaine*. This was "the day of the year" among the Pagan Irish, the 1st of January being adopted with Christianity. O'Reilly writes *céideamh* and *céideamhain*. O'Donovan's Grammar (p. 97) gives *ceideamh* as the nominative form. The word is from *ceud*, first, and *Samh*, summer, the oblique forms being *ceudshamhan* and *ceudshamhain*. The second great anniversary was *Oidhche Samhna*, or "All Hallow Eve," as it was afterwards called. Samhain is from *samh* and *fuin*, end of summer (see Book of Rights Introd., p. lii.). Thus the year was divided into two great equal portions, which were each subdivided in the same way, making four *ratha*, or quarters. The months were not introduced until St. Patrick's time.

b. Cuċt, *color*, *gl*. ʋaċ, color, *gl*. cuınnρe, *gl*. ɜné, face, countenance, mien.—O'D.

c. Cáí, *gl*. cuaċs, cuckoos.—O'D.

d. Cρuaıḃ, *constant*, *gl*. ʋıan.—O'D.

e. [*Sámh-shuaill*]. *Summer suaill*, *gl*. the swallows. The words of this fragment, which was considered to be the first composition of Fionn, after having eaten the salmon of the Boyne, are very ancient and exceedingly obscure. The translation is only offered for the consideration of Irish scholars, for it is certain that the meaning of some of the lines is doubtful. The poem obviously wants some lines at the end ; and Mr. Cleaver states, that the remaining portion of the manuscript is so defaced as to render it totally illegible.—O'D.

f. *Sigine*. This word is very doubtful, in fact illegible, and the meaning assigned to it cannot be received. Surely the stars were not called by the early Irish *signa* or signs.

The map accompanying this edition will be found very useful to the student and interesting to the general reader as affording a very fair idea of the physical outlines of Ireland in the third century. The borders of the four subkingdoms or provinces, which, with the mensal province of the Airdrigh, made up the Irish Pentarchy, are shown by the blue line as well as can be ascertained, for they varied much at different times, and often within short intervals. The track followed by Fionn in his exploits is shown by the **green** line with the different scenes indicated. His track in **the pursuit** of Diarmuid and Grainne, as well **as the course of the two** fugitives, **is** pointed out by the red **line, and the** places mentioned **in the** account of their **wanderings are all** marked. **Many** other spots mentioned **in the annals and romances of the same** period are also shown, including **the most** remarkable places in ancient Irish history.

P. W. Joyce, LL.D., and Mr. John Fleming have read **a** great **part** of this work while going through the press, and their remarks have been in the main availed of by the editor, who, while venturing here and there to differ from their judgment, has yet to express his thanks for the great care given to the reading of the proofs, and for many valuable hints.

# LETTER

### ADDRESSED BY DR. JOHN O'DONOVAN TO THE PRESIDENT OF THE OSSIANIC SOCIETY.

DUBLIN, *Dec. 27th*, 1858.

DEAR SIR,—Having, at your **request,** undertaken **to** translate into English—to lengthen **out the** abbreviations, **and to** fix the grammatical endings **of** the contracted **words, in this** notice of the boyish exploits of the celebrated Fionn Mac Chumhaill, the "Fingal" of Mac Pherson's "Ossian,"*—I beg **to** offer **you** a few observations **on the age**

---

* In the facsimiles **of portions of** ancient Gaelic MSS. relating to Fionn, preserved in Scotland, some of which were published in the Highland Society's "Report on Ossian," the name of the great chief of the Fiann is written Find, Fint, and Finn (Ua Baeiscne), as in this and every old Irish writing; which ought **to** be conclusive that MacPherson had no authority for naming him Fingal. That form is not found in any ancient writing, and most probably is merely a vulgar blending of Fionn's name, and that of his father, Cumhall.

and importance of the little tract, as well as of the manuscript from which it has been taken. This tract was copied, letter for letter, and contraction for contraction, from a fragment of the Psalter of Cashel, now preserved in the Bodleian Library at Oxford (*Laud.* 610), by the Rev. Euseby D. Cleaver, M.A., of Christ Church, Oxford, in 1854, and now curate of S. Barnabas, Pimlico, London,* whose progress in the study of the Irish language is truly wonderful, considering the very slight advantages of oral instruction which he possessed. He has copied this little tract so faithfully that I was able to understand it as well as if I had the original manuscript before me. No artist ever copied a portrait or inscription more accurately. This manuscript was examined in the year 1844 by the Rev. Dr. Todd, S.F.,T.C.D., who published a full account of its contents in the "Proceedings of the Royal Irish Academy," vol. 2, p. 336 sq. In 1846, I examined it again with the most anxious care, and published a brief notice of its more important contents in the introduction to Leabhar na g-Ceart.† It consists of 292 pages, folio, vellum, and was transcribed, in 1453, by John Boy O'Clery and others at Pottlerath, in the barony of Crannagh, and county of Kilkenny, for Edmund Butler, the head of the sept of Mac Richard, who afterwards became Earls of Ormonde. This manuscript remained in the possession of Mac Richard Butler till the year 1462, when Ormonde and he were defeated in a battle fought at Baile-an-phoill, now Pilltown, in the barony of Iverk, county of Kilkenny, by Thomas, Earl of Desmond, to whom he was obliged to give up this very copy of the Psalter of Cashel, together with another manuscript (now unknown), called the Book of Carrick-on-Suir. This fact appears from a memorandum on fol. 110, p. b, of which the following is a literal translation:—

"This was the Psalter of Mac Richard Butler, until the defeat at Baile-an-phoill was given to the Earl of Ormonde and to Mac Richard by the Earl of Desmond (Thomas); when this book and the book of Carrick were obtained in the redemption of Mac Richard; and it was this Mac

* **Now** (1881) Rector of Laindon Hills, Romford, Essex. To Rev Mr. Cleaver the thanks of the present editor are due for his courtesy in furnishing every information in his power concerning this MS., when communicated with. He was also one of the earliest to come forward in generous support and encouragement of the Gaelic Union.

† See pp. xxii-xxxiii., "Book of Rights," published for the "Celtic Society."

Richard that had these books transcribed for his own use; and they remained in his possession until Thomas, Earl of Desmond, wrested them from him."

The foregoing memorandum was written in the manuscript, while it was in the possession of Thomas, Earl of Desmond, whose name, "Thomas, of Desmond," appears in English, in his own hand, on fol. 92, a. (See *Leabhar na g-Ceart*, Introduction, pp. xxviii.-xxx.) The publication of this manuscript, as it stands, would be a great desideratum in Irish literature, and I trust that Sir John Romilly* will not think it unworthy of his attention.

I am of opinion that this little tract is of great antiquity, and contains, perhaps, the oldest account we have remaining of Fionn and his contemporaries. You will observe that the style is extremely simple, and altogether devoid of that redundancy of epithets which characterises the prose compositions of later ages which are equalled only by those of "*El famoso Feliciano de Silva*."

The celebrated Irish antiquary, Duald Mac Firbis, in his genealogical work, pp. 435, 436, gives various pedigrees of the famous Irish hero, Fionn son of Cumhall. Some deduce his descent from the Orbhraighe of Druim Imnocht, others from the Corca Oiche, a sept of the Ui-Fidhgeinte, who were seated in the present county of Limerick. Some state that he sprung from the Ui-Tairsigh of Ui-Failghe, a plebeian sept, while other genealogists maintain that he came of the Ui-Tairsigh of the Luaighni Teamhrach of *Fera-Cul* in Bregia, which was one of the three septs from whom the chief leader of the Fiann, or Irish militia, was elected. Mac Firbis, however, states that this discrepancy must have arisen from mistaking one Fionn for another; but that by far the greater number of the authentic Irish authorities agree in deducing the pedigree of the famous Fionn Mac Chumhaill from Nuada Neacht, the fourth son of Sedna Sithbhaic, the ancestor of the kings of Leinster.

By the mother's side, Fionn Mac Chumhaill was descended from Tadhg, son of Nuadhat, son of Aice, son of Daite, son of Brocan, son of Fintan of Tuath-Daite in Bregia. This Mac Firbis believes to be his true maternal descent, though others state that his mother was Torba,

* Then the Master of the Rolls in England, under whose direction the Commission for the publication of the "Chronicles and Memorials of Great Britain and Ireland during the Middle Ages," issues its publications. Several very valuable Irish works have been published by this Commission, but not, as yet, the MS. referred to.

daughter of Eochoman of the Ernaans of Dun-Cearmna (the old head of Kinsale, in the county of Cork),* and that he had a half-brother by the mother's side, who was called Fionn Mac Gleoir.†

Mac Firbis adds that Fionn Mac Chumhaill possessed, in right of his office of leader of the Fiann, seven ballys, or townlands, out of every triocha-ched, or hundred in Ireland; that he was born in the third year of the reign of Conn *Céadchathach*, and died in the year 283.

Some genealogical books give the pedigree of our hero thus:—Fionn, son of Cumhall, son of Trenmor, son of Subalt, son of Ealtan, son of Baiscue, son of Nuada Necht: others, Fionn, son of Cumhall. son of Baiscne, son of Trenmor, son of Ferdarath, son of Goll, son of Forgall, son of Daire, son of Deaghaidh, son of Sin; but of the various pedigrees of our hero, which Mac Firbis has copied from Irish authorities, the following is the only one that can be considered authentic:—

1. Nuada Necht,
2. Fergus Failge, ancestor of the Kings of Leinster,
3. Rossa Ruadh,
4. Finn, the poet, King of Leinster,
5. Conchobhar Abhraruadh,
6. Moghcorb, King of Leinster,
7. Cucorb, King of Leinster,
8. Nia Corb,
9. Cormac Gealtagaoith,
10. Feilimidh Firurglais,
11. Cathaeir Mor, Monarch of Ireland, A.D., 177.

3. So-alt,
4. Alt,
5. Cairbre Garbhroin,
6. Baeiscne,
7. Modh,
8. Buan,
9. Fergus,
10. Trendorn,
11. Trenmor,
12. Cumhall,
13. Fionn Mac Chumhaill, slain, 284.

He had a sister named Sidh, who was proverbial in Ireland for her fleetness of foot, and who was the mother of Caoilte son of Ronan, also famous in the Fenian tales for his agility. He had another sister, Seogen, who was the mother of Cobhthach, son of Crunnchu.

I have always believed that Fionn Mac Chumhaill was a real historical personage and not a myth or god of war, like the Hercules of the Greeks, the Odin of the Scan-

* See note, par. 2. It would seem from part of that note that "Teamhair Earann" was situated in a different locality.
† This is he to whom reference is made in paragraph 13.

dinavians, or the Siegfried of the Germans. He was the son-in-law of the famous Cormac son of Art, Monarch of Ireland, and the general of his standing army. He was slain in the year A.D., 284, according to the Annals of Tighernach, a period to which our authentic history unquestionably reaches. (See *Ogygia*, part iii., c. 70.)

This celebrated warrior was, as we have seen, of the regal line of the kings of Leinster, of the Milesian or Scotic race (for my ingenious friend, Mr. Herbert F. Hore, has theorized in vain to prove him of Scandinavian origin); he had two residences in Leinster, one at Allen (Almha), in the present county of Kildare,* and the other at Moyelly in the (now) King's County, both of which descended to him from his ancestors.† Pinkerton, the most critical and sceptical writer that has ever treated of Irish and Scottish history, has the following remarkable words, in which he expresses his conviction of Fionn's undoubted historical existence:—

"He seems," says he, "to have been a man of great talents for the age, and of celebrity in arms. His formation of a regular standing army, trained to war, in which all the Irish accounts agree, seems to have been a rude imitation of the Roman legions in Britain. The idea, though simple enough, shows prudence, for such a force alone could have coped with the Romans had they invaded Ireland. But this machine, which surprised a rude age, and seems the basis of all Finn's fame, like some other great schemes, only lived in its author, and expired soon after him."—*Inquiry into the History of Scotland*, vol. ii., p. 77.

Our own poet and historian, Moore, who read all that had been written by Mac Pherson and modern critics on the history of Fionn, expresses his conviction that he was a real man of flesh and blood, and no god of war or poetical creation. He concludes his account of him in the following poetical strain:—

"It has been the fate of this popular Irish hero, after a long

* There are two hills (so-called) of "Allen," one the ancient seat of the Kings of Leinster, called *Dún-áilinne*, near old Kilcullen; the other the more celebrated head-quarters of the Fiann, about seven miles to the north-west, called *Cnoc-almhan*. From the latter of these hills is named the "Bog of Allen." Both were among the largest forts in the country, and occupied very commanding positions. The great moat and remains of the ramparts of Dún-áilinne are still visible.

† Miss Brooke says that it was in right of his mother, Muireann Múnchaomh, who was daughter of Tadhg, son of Nuadha, and second wife of Cumhall, that Fionn possessed his palace of Almha. See O'Curry's "Magh Léana" (Introduction, p. x.) for the origin of the name Almha.

course of traditional renown in his own country, where his name still lives, not only in legends and songs, but in the yet more indelible record of scenery connected with his memory, to have been all at once transferred by adoption to another country (Scotland), and start, under a new but false shape, in a fresh career of fame."—*History of Ireland,* vol. i., p. 133.

The only descendants of our hero, now known to exist, are the Dal Cais, *i., e.* O'Briens of Munster and their co-relatives. Cormac Cas, King of Munster, married Samhair the daughter of Fionn by Grainne, daughter of Cormac, son of Art, Monarch of Ireland, and had by her, according to the Irish genealogists, three sons, Tinne and Connla, of whose race nothing is known, and Fearcorb, the progenitor of the Dal Cais, the hereditary enemies of the race of Conn. After the death of Fionn, the monarch Cairbre Liffeachar, son of Cormac the grandson of Conn, disbanded and outlawed the Clanna Baeiscne, of whom Fionn was then the head, and retained in his service their enemies, the Clanna Morna, a military tribe of the Firbolg of Connacht. The Clanna Baeiscne then repaired to Munster to their relative, Fearcorb, who retained them in his service, contrary to the orders of the monarch. This led to the bloody battle of Gabhra (near the Boyne in Meath), in which the two rival military tribes slaughtered each other almost to extermination.* In the heat of the action, Oscar, the grandson of Fionn (and son of Oisin), met the monarch in single combat ; but fell, and the monarch, retiring from the combat, was met by his own relative, Semeon, one of the Fotharta (a tribe that had been expelled into Leinster),† who fell upon him after having been severely wounded in the dreadful combat with Oscar, and despatched him by a single blow.

Oisin and Caoilte survived all the followers of our hero, and are fabled to have lived down to the time of St. Patrick (A.D. 432), to whom they related the wonderful exploits of Fionn and his contemporaries.‡ This, how-

* The Fiann seem to have resembled very closely the Praetorian guards of old Rome ; Almha was to Teamhair what the Praetorian camp was to the city of the Cæsars. The Fianna Eireann did not indeed set up and pull down kings, but, from being at first a protection to the monarchy they became in the end a source of apprehension so great that the whole force of the Airdrigh aided by their rivals was put forward to crush them.

† This tribe gave name to the Barony of " Forth," south of Wexford.

‡ See " Agallamh Oisin agus Phádraic " in Miss Brooke's " Chase

ever, is incredible ; but it is highly probable that both lived to converse with some Christian missionaries who preceded the great apostle of Ireland, and who found it difficult to convert them from their pagan notions.

There is a very curious dialogue, partly preserved in the Book of Lismore, and partly in a MS. in the Bodleian Library at Oxford, said to have been carried on between Caeilte, son of Ronan, and St. Patrick.* This dialogue, notwithstanding its anachronism, or perhaps rather misnomer, is of great value to the Irish linguist, topographer, and antiquary, on account of the curious ancient forms of the language which it preserves, and the various forts, mounds, sepulchres, plains, mountains, estuaries and rivers which it mentions by their primitive and mediæval names.

Hoping that this tract will soon see the light under your auspices, as President of our Society,

I remain, dear Sir,

Yours very truly,
JOHN O'DONOVAN.

To
WILLIAM SMITH O'BRIEN ESQ.,
*President of the Ossianic Society.*

---

of Sliabh Guillion," or in the fourth volume of the Ossianic Society. See also " Laoidh Oisin air Thir na n-óg," or the " Lay of Oisin on the land of the Young," published for the Gaelic Union.

* It is now pretty generally held that Christianity was known to some in Ireland before St. Patrick's arrival, and probably from a very early period. The part filled by some of the first teachers of the faith in the dialogues said to have been held with the ancient men of Eire, may, naturally enough, have been ascribed to St. Patrick, whose fame eclipses that of his predecessors.

# VOCABULARY.

ᴀ, *interj.* (*sign of voc. case*). O.
ᴀ (or ᴅo) *sign of inf. mood*, **to**.
ᴀ, *poss. pron.*, his, her, its, **their**.
ᴀ or ɪ, *prep.*, in ; ᴀ ɢ-ceᴀnn, in (or at) the head or end.
ᴀ, *rel. pron.*, who, which, that, all that.
ᴀ *for* ó, *prep.*, from, *q. v.*
ᴀb, *subj. form of* ɪꞅ, *assertive verb*, is ; ᴅ'ᴀ n-ᴀb *or* ᴅ'ᴀ ꞃ -ᴀb, to whom or which is : *see* buᴅ.
ᴀc, *see* ᴀɢ.
ᴀcᴀ, *pr. pron.*, at them : cɪᴀ ᴀcᴀ, which of them. (*Idiom*.)
ᴀcc, *obs. neg. par.*, **no, not**.
ᴀccᴀ, *obs. form of* ꝼᴀcᴀɪᴅ, *q. v.*
ᴀccᴀɪb, *obs. form of* ꝼáɢ, *q. v.*
ᴀccᴀɪnn, *see* ᴀɢᴀɪnn.
ᴀċᴛ, *conj.* but ; ᴀċᴛ ċeᴀnᴀ, however.
ᴀccu, *see* ᴀcᴀ.
ᴀᴅ, *obs. par. before verbs* : *see* ᴀᴛ *and* ᴅo.
ᴀᴅbeꞃcɪꞅ, *obs. verb*, used to say (*hab. past*) : *see* ɢᴀɪꞃɪᴅɪꞅ, used to call ; *and* ᴅeɪꞃ, say.
ᴀᴅnᴀɪɢ, *obs. verb*, gave, went : *see* ᴀᴛnᴀɢᴀᴅ.
ᴀeᴅ, *see* ᴀoḋ.
ᴀen, *see* ᴀon.
ᴀenuꞃ, *see* ᴀonᴀꞃ.
ᴀeꞅ, *see* ᴀoꞅ.
ᴀɢ, *sign of pres. part.*, **at**.
ᴀɢ, *prep.*, at, with, to, *see* ᴀɪɢ.
ᴀɢ, *obs. n. m.*, a wild cow or deer, ᴀɢᴀɪb, *dat. pl.*
áɢ, *obs. n. m.*, *gen.* áɪɢ, valour ; cóɪṁċɪonól áɪɢ, a **meeting of valour** (used adjectively.)
ᴀɢᴀɪb, *dat. pl.*, *see* ᴀɢ.
ᴀɢᴀɪᴅ, *see* ᴀɢᴀɪḋ.
ᴀɢᴀɪḋ, *n. f., gen.* -ᴅe, *pl.* ᴀɪɢċe; a face ; ᴀ n-ᴀɢᴀɪḋ, against ; 'nᴀ (*or* ɪ n-ᴀ) ᴀɢᴀɪḋ, against him : ᴀɪꞃ ᴀɢᴀɪḋ, forward. (*Idioms.*)

againn, *pr. pron.*, at us, with us : ᵹan againn, stay with us ; ᵽaᵽcuᵹaḋ againn, to keep with us.
agam, *pr. pron.*, at **me,** with me.
aguᵽ, *conj.*, and.
aicce }
aice  } *see* aici.
aici, *pr. pron.*, at or with her.
aicill, *obs. n., f. gen.* aicle, watch, ᵽoᵽ aicill, in wait : *see* aiᵽ ci, *and note, par.* 32.
áiġ, *see* áġ.
aiġ, *prep.*, at ; *see* aġ.
aiġe, *pr. pron.*, at him ; aiġe-ᵽean, *emph. form.*
aiġi, *see* aiġe.
aile, *see* eile.
aileḋ, *see* oil.
aill, *obs. form of* eile, *q. v.*
áille, *n. f. gen., id.* beauty, brilliance.
ailᵽec, *see* oil.
aimᵽiġ, *v. a.*, aim, direct ; aimᵽiġeaᵽ, *hist. pres. tense.*
aimᵽiġeaᵽ, *see* aimᵽiġ.
ainḃᵽioᵽ, *n. m., gen.* -ᵽeaᵽa, ignorance ; *from* an *negative, and* ᵽioᵽ : 'na ainḃᵽioᵽ, unknown to him.
aine, *obs. n.*, force, vehemence ; co n-aine, le bᵽiġ, with force ; compare aine ceneaḋ, in *Luireach Phádraig.*
ainᵽiᵽ, *see* ainḃᵽioᵽ.
ainim, *see* ainm.
ainm, *n. m., gen.* anma, *pl.* anmanna, a name ; Fionn ḋ'ainm, Fionn (is) thy name. *See note on par.* 12.
aiᵽ *or* aᵽ, *prep.* on ; aiᵽ bić, *see* bić ; aiᵽ cí, *see* cí.
aiᵽ, *pr. pron.*, on him, *or* it.
aiᵽ, *for* óiᵽ, *prep.*, for.
aiᵽe, *n. m.*, cause, occasion ; also heed, attention.
aiᵽeaṁ, *n. m., gen.* -ᵽiṁ, number.
aiᵽiᵽ, *see* aᵽiᵽ.
aiᵽᵽi, *or* uiᵽᵽi, *pr. pron.*, on her.
áic, *n. f., gen. and pl.* áice, a place.
aiċeaċ, *n. m., gen.* -ċiġ, a peasant, a rustic.
aiċhiġ, *see* aiċeaċ.
alba, *p. n. f, gen.* -bann, *dat.* -bainn, Scotland.
albann, *see* alba.
allca, *adj.* wild.
alluiḋ, *obs. adj.* wild.
alma, *obs. n.*, a herd, a drove.
álṁa, *n. f., gen.* álṁan ; *Cnoc-Álmhan,* Fionn's residence : *see note, p.* 74.

**ałmuin,** *n. f.,* gen. -ine; *Dún-Almhuine or Dún-áilinne,* the ancient seat of the kings of Leinster: *see note, p.* 74.

**altrum,** *obs.* nursed, reared.

**am,** *n. m.* time; ann an am ſin, in (or at) that time.

**am',** *pr. pron.,* in my: *for* ann mo.

**amać,** *adv.* out (*with verbs of motion and action*) do ċuaiḋ ſe amaċ, he went out; cuir amaċ, put out.

**amach,** *see* amaċ.

**amail,** *adj.* like; *adv.* how.

**amlaiḋ,** *adv.* like, thus; iſ amlaiḋ ſo, it is in this manner.

**amlaid,** *see* amlaiḋ.

**amraine,** *see* amraine.

**amraine,** *n. m.* military service (as a mercenary soldier.)

**an,** *art., n. and g. m.*; na, *gen. f., and pl. m. and f.,* the.

**anaenfeaċt,** *see* aoinfeaċt.

**anam,** *n. m.,* gen. anama, life, also the soul; gan anam, lifeless.

**and,** *see* ann.

**anmanda,** *see* ainm.

**anmanna,** *see* ainm.

**anmuin,** *obs. form of* anam, *q. v.*

**ann,** *prep.* in, into.

**ann,** *pr. pron.* in him, *or* it.

**ann,** *adv.* there; *lit.* in it; ann ſo, here (in this); ann ſúd, there (yonder); ann ſin (in that), there, then; lá eile ann, a certain other day.

**anns,** *prep.* (form of ann), in; anns an g-caṫ, in the battle.

**Aoḋ,** *p. n. m.,* Aodh, a man's name.

**aoinfeaċt,** *cpd. n.,* one time; a n-aoinfeaċt, in one time; a n-aoinfeaċt le, together with.

**aois,** *n. f., gen.* aoise, age.

**aon,** *num. adj.,* one, any, a; aonṁná, of a woman; m'aon ṁac, my only son; mar aon, as one, together; mar aon le, together with.

**aonar,** *n. m.,* one man (like triuir, ceatrar, &c.); 'na aonar, in his one-man, alone.

**aon-ṁná,** *cpd. n. f. gen.,* of one woman; gul na h-aon-ṁná, the cry of the one woman, who must have been some mysterious personage.

**aos,** *n. m.,* folk, people; aos óg, the young folk; aos ceardḋa, folk of trade, artisans, artificers; *also,* poets (here most likely the meaning) as poetry was *the* art or *ceard:* aos dána, poets.

**ar,** *prep.,* on, upon, *see* air.

**ar,** *def. v.,* says, said, quoth; arſa miſe, *emph.,* says I.

ap, *obs. form of* óip, *q. v.*
apaile, } *adv. obs.* other, **another,** *equivalent to* " *et cetera;*"
apoile, } *see* eile.
ápo, *adj., comp.* áipoe *and* aoipoe, high, tall, chief, head.
ápomaepaizcéc, *see* ápomaopacc.
ápomaopacc, *cpd. n. f.*, high-stewardship.
apír, *or* aipír, *adv.*, again.
ar, *see* ir.
ar, *pr. pron.*, out of him, *or* it.
ar, *prep.*, out of; ar rin, from that; ar ro, hence.
arna, *n. m.* a rib.
arnac, *adj.*, ribbed; ceann-arnac, strong-ribbed.
arcaio, *see* rarcuiz.
arcuo, *see* rarcuiz.
ac. *obs. par.*, *see p.* 57; *also* ac *and* oo.
ác, *n. m.*, *gen.* áca, a ford.
acá, *see* cá.
acaip, *n. m.*, *gen.* acap, a father; oeapbpácaip a acaip, his father's brother.
acáic, *obs. v.*, *see* cá.
Ác-an-béil-oeirg, *p. n. m.*, *Ford of the redmouthed one.*
acap, *gen.*, *see* acaip.
acbepc, *obs. v.*, said: *see* oubaipc.
accuip, *see* accuip.
accuip, *v. a., inf.* accup, put, offer, bring, give.
ac rec, *def. obs. v. impers.* he relates.
áczlonoa, *p. n. m.*, *Athglonda*, Glonda's ford.
acnazac, *obs. v.*, they bring, go; *see note, par.* 25.
acnuiz, *see* aonaiz.
acracc, *obs. v.* rises, goes.
b', *see* buó *or* ba.
ba, it was: *see* buó; ba h-aimn, was name; co m-ba, until was; ba. *obs.* was; *see* ba and bi; ro ba *for* oo bí. ba is still used in Scotland.
baó *(cond. of* ir*) asser .v.*, it would be; *also past: see* buó; zo m-baó, that it may be.
báoio, *see* báioió *and* báió.
báz, } *n. m. obs., gen.* báiz, strength, power; co ro-baiz, with
baz, } great power.
báió, *v. ac.*, drown; báioió re, he drowns; oo baió, drowned *(past.)*
báio, *see* báió.
báio, *see* báió.
báioió, *see* báió.
baiz, *see* báz.

baile, *n. m., pl.* -lte, a town, place, townland; gur an m-baile ceudna, to the same place: a baile, *or* 'ra m-bailo, home, at home.

bain, *prefix: see* ban.

baincéile, *n. f.* a wife, *from* ban *or* bain, *fem. prefix*, and céile, a companion.

bain-féinnibe, *n. f.* a heroine, an amazon; do na bain-féinnroib, *dat. pl.*

ban, *prefix*, written bain before a slender vowel, changes the gender of the noun to which it is prefixed; so the feminine of **any noun** may be formed.

bán, *adj., comp. and gen. f.* báine, white.

banb Sionna, *p. n. m.: see note, par.* 11.

ban-cele, *see* bain-céile.

ban-dpai, *see* ban-dpaoi.

ban-dpaoi, *n. f.* a Druidess.

ban-féinoio } *old dative form: see* bain-féinnibe.
ban-féinoig }

ban-féinoeouib, *old dative pl.*: *see* bain-féinnibe.

bápac, } *obs.* morrow; *see* mápac; and note par. 25.
bápach, } air n-a m-bápac, air an mápac, on the
báipech, } morrow.

bátar, *obs.* they were; *see* under bí.

batur, *see* bátar.

bean, *n. f., gen. and pl.* mná; *dat.* mnaoi; *gen. pl.* ban, a woman, a wife (*see* baincéile); na h-aon-mná, *see* note, par. 44.

beanntraige, *p. n. f.* Bantry: *see note, par.* 33c.

béarfad-ra, *see* beirim.

beirbead *v. subs. cond.*, would be; dá m-beirbead (dá m-beich), it could or should be.

beir, *v. ac. irr. imp.*, bring forth, bear, carry; beirear ri mac (*hist. pres.*) she bears a son: beirid, they bear; beirid re leir, he brings with him; beirid leo, they bring off with them; do beirbead re, he used to bring.

beirbead, *see* beir.

beirear, *see* beir.

beirear, *see* beirim.

beirid, *see* beir.

beirid, *see* beirim.

beirid, *for* beirib, *see* beirear *and* beirib.

beirim, *v. irr. pres. indic.*, I give; beir, gives, wins; 3rd pers.: beirear, *hist. pres.* gives; beirtear, *pres. pass.* is given, fought, won; beirid, *pl.* they give, they send; béarfad-ra, *fut. emph.* I will give.

beiɼċeaɼ, *see* beiɼim.
beiċ, *v. sub.* (vo *or* a beiċ, *inf. of* ċáim) to be; beiċ, *or* aᵹ beiċ, being; a beiċ aici, his being with her; é beiċ annɼ an ionav úv, he to be in that place.
beiṫ, *for* beiveaḋ, *cond. q. v.*
bél, *for* beul.
ben *for* bean.
benṫɼaiᵹe, *for* beannṫɼaiᵹe.
beo, *adj.*, *gen. m.* bí, *f.* beo *and* beoiċe, alive, living; v'ḟan beo, who remained alive; an beo, the living (the name of the enchanted pig.) *See p.* 37.
beolu, *for* beul, *q. v.*
béɼ, *for* beáɼfav, *q. v.*
beɼa, *obs.*; *see* beiɼ.
beɼaiv, *for* beiɼiv; *see* beiɼ.
beɼaiṫ, *for* beiɼiṫ; *s e* beiɼ.
beɼaɼ, *obs.*, *see* beiɼċeaɼ.
beɼev, *for* beiɼiḋ; *see* beiɼ *and* beiɼim.
beɼṫ. *for* beiɼ, *or* ṫuᵹ.
beċ, *obs.*, *see* beiċ.
beul, *n. m.*, *gen. and pl.* béil, a mouth; beul-ḋeaɼᵹ, *cpd. adj.* red-mouthed; an béil ḋeiɼᵹ, of the red mouth; am' beul, in my mouth.
beul-ḋeaɼᵹ, *see* beul.
bí, *for* bí.
bí, *for* biḋ.
bí, *v. sub.*, *imp.* be.
bí, *v. subs. past indic.*, was; biḋeavaɼ (báṫaɼ), they were.
biḋ, *v. sub.*, *hab. pres.* is (does be), is in the habit of being; aiɼ a m-biḋ (ɼoɼɼ a m-bí), on which is usually.
biḋeaḋ, *v. sub.*, *hab. past*, used to be, was; ᵹo m-biḋeaḋ ɼe, that he used to be; vo biḋeaḋ, which used to be.
biḋeann, *hab. pres.* (*see* biḋ), is.
biṫ, } *n. f.*, existence, the world; aiɼ biṫ, *or* 'ɼa m-biṫ, any, biṫ, } any in life, at all.
blav, *for* bláḋ.
bláḋ, *n. m.*, *obs.*, renown, fame (*see* bláċ) (co m-bláḋ, *see* note, *par.* 6a.)
bláḋma, *p. n. f.*, a personage in Irish story, from whom Sliabh Bladhma takes its name.
blaiv, *for* bláḋ.
blaċ, *for* bláċ.
bláċ, *n. m.*, *gen. and pl.* bláċa, a bossom, a flower; (ṫuiᵹṫeaɼ bláċa an biṫ, the earth is covered with flowers).

bláṫa, see bláṫ.
bláċuiġ, *v. ac. and n.* blossom; blaċuiġiḋ, 3*rd pers. pres. tense,* blossoms, flourishes.
bláċuiġiḋ, *see* bláċuiġ.
bliaḋain, *n. f., gen.* bliaḋna; *pl.* bliaḋana *and* bliaḋanta, a year; a g-ceann ré m-bliaḋan, at the end of six years; bliaḋain go leiṫ, a year and a half.
bliaḋan, *see* bliaḋain.
bliaḋna, *pl., see* bliaḋain.
bó. *n. f., g.n. id., dat.* boin, *pl.* ba, *dat. pl.* buaib, a cow.
bo, *for* ba.
bóḋṁall, *p. n. f.* **Bodhmhall, a Druidess.**
boḋhmall, *for* bóḋṁall.
boi, *for* ba *and* biḋeaḋ, *q. v.*
boin, *dat.*, *see* bó.
boinn, *p. n. f., gen.* boinne, the River Boyne.
boiṫ, *dat., see* boṫ.
**bolg,** *n. m., gen. and pl.* builg *or* boilg, a bag; copp-bolg, a round bag or purse (of jewels, charms, &c.)
bolgaċ, *gen.* -aiġe, *n. f.* the smallpox; *n. m.* a boil; *gen.* -aiġ, *pl.*, bolgaiġe, blains, boils, **blisters.**
bolgaiġe, *see* bolgaċ.
boṫ, *n. f., gen.* boiṫe, *dat.* boiṫ, *pl.* boṫa, a **tent, a booth,** a hut; fiann-boṫ, a hunting booth in the forest.
**bórd,** *n. m., gen. and pl.* bóird, a board, a border; air imeal-bórd, on the bordering shore.
braḋán, *n. m., gen. and pl.* -áin, a salmon; *see* eo.
braḋan, *for* braḋán.
brec, *for* breug.
**breug,** *n. f., gen.* bréige, *pl.*, breuga, a lie; ní breug ó, it is no lie.
**briġ,** *n. f., gen.* briġe, strength, vigour; le briġ (co n-áine), with agility.
bruinne, *n. obs.*, a brink, margin, limit. (*See* O'Donovan's Supplement to O'Reilly's Dictionary, *in voce.*)
bu, *see* buḋ.
buaib, *dat. pl.; see* bó.
buaiḋ, *n. f., gen.* buaiḋe, *pl.* buaḋa, victory; na **m-buaḋ,** *see note, par.* 10.
buaid, *for* buaiḋ.
buan, *adj., comp.,* buaine, lasting: fíorbuan, steadfast.
buḋ, *assertive verb, past tense,* it was; *written also* ba; (*obsolete forms,* bo, boi, bui, fa, &*c.*)
bui, *see* buḋ.
buile, *n. obs.; see* bolgaċ.

bup, *poss. pron. pl.* your.
cá, *int. part*, what ; cá h-ainm, what name.
ca, *see* cia.
các, *indef. pron. ; gen.* cáic, everyone, all.
cac, *for* gac, *q. v.*
cach, *for* các.
cad, *int. adv.* what.
caem, *for* caom, *q. v.*
caempamaip, *v. obs.* we can.
caí, *obs. ; see note, par.* 56c.
cáic, *gen. of* các, *q. v.*
caill, *for* coill, *q. v.*
caille, *for* coille ; *see* coill.
cáin, *for* caoin, *q. v.*
Caipbpe, *p. n. m.*, Cairbre.
Caipbpige, *p. n. f.*, Cairbrighe, *see note, par.* 35.
Caipbpige, *see* Caipbpige.
Caipppe, *see* Caipbpe.
Caipeal, *p. n. m., gen.* -il, Caiseal, Cashel.
Caipil, *gen., see* Caipeal.
can, *v.* sing ; po can *or* do can, sang ; canait, *for* canaid, they sing ; amail po can, as sang ; Fionn po can ( t was) Fionn who sang.
canac, *n.*, name of a plant : bog-down, *also* cotton-down.
canaid, *see* can.
canait, *see* can.
caoin, *adj.*, pleasing, mild ; caoin-pe, delightful time.
caoin-pe, *see* caoin.
caom, *adj.*, beautiful, graceful, gentle.
cappac, *n. m.* a bald-head ; *adj.* mangy.
cappach, *see* cappac.
cat, *n. m., gen.* cata, a battle ; a g-cat, in battle.
cata, *gen. of* cat.
cath, *see* cat.
cath-plog, *see* cat-fluag.
cat-fluag, *cpd., n. m.* battle-host.
cead, *n. m.*, leave ; tabaip cead, give leave.
céad, *num. adj.*, a hundred ; na g-céad, of the hundreds ; na g-céad ngníom, of the hundreds of exploits.
ceann. *n. m., gen. and pl.* cinn (1), a head : the end : a g-ceann peactmaine, at the end of a week ;—pe m-bliadain,—of six years ; ceannaib, *dat. pl.* (2), a single one, one head, an individual ; ceann aca, one of them.
ceannaib, *dat. pl. see* ceann.

ceana, *adv.* even, already, nevertheless, else; oléeana, likewise; act ceana, however; a n-eipinn ceana, in Eire anywhere; *see* O'Donovan's Supplement to Dictionary, p. 595.

ceann-bán, *cpd. adj.*, head-white; *i.e.*, **white-headed**; *n. m.* name of a plant, *also* ceanaban; *see* canac.

ceapoa, *see* céipoe *and* céipo.

ceapoai, *see* céipo.

ceatpama, *n. f., gen.* -man, *pl.* -mna, a quarter, the fourth.

cech, *for* gac, *q. v.*

ceo *or* céo, *for* céao *or* ceuo, *q. v.*

ceona *or* ceonai, *obs., for* ceuona, *q. v.*

céile, *n. m. and f.*, a companion, a spouse; a céile, *pron*, each other; map a céile, as its fellow, likewise; or gac papac ann a céile, from one desert to the other.

céileabpap, *see* céileabpaio.

céileabpaio, *v. ac. def.* to bid farewell; céileabpap, *hist. pres. tense*, takes leave.

céipo, *n. f., gen.* céipoe, trade, art, *also* poetry; (*see notes, par.* 20 *a. and p.* 68); aor céipoe, artificers.

céle, *for* céile, *q. v.*

celebpao, *for* ceileabpaio, *q. v.*

celebpaio-pim, *obs. for* ceileabpaio péipean, **he** bids farewell, takes leave; *also* converses.

cen, *for* gan, *q. v.*

cena, *see* ceana.

ceno, *see* ceann.

cenn, *see* ceann.

cenb, ceapb, } *obs. n.*, a lappet, a rag, a border, a fringe; bpuinne cenb caill cpaib, the margin-fringe of branching woods; *see* coill.

cenbuio, ceapbaio, } *obs. v.*, they skim or glide over; ceapbaio rnuc, they touch with **their wings** the surface of the stream.

cencat, *obs. v.*; they aim.

cettemain, *obs. n., see* céioeam, *and* ceuopam.

céioeam, *n. f., gen.* -eaman, *dat.*, eamain; May-day, the month of May; *i.e.*, ceuopam, first of summer; *q. v.*

cet, *obs. for* can, *q. v.*; po cet, *i.e.* po can, sang.

cethpaime *for* ceatpama, *q. v.*

ceuo. *num. adj.*, first; ir é ceuo goin, for which we would now say, ir é goin air o-túr, it is he who wounded first (Cumhall), *see par.* 47.

ceuo-pam, *n. f., gen.* -man, *dat.* -main, May-day, the month of May; *see* céioeam *and note a. on par.* 56.

ceuḋna, *ind. adj.* same; map an ġ-ceuḋna, as the same, likewise.

chum, *see* ċum.

chuaiḋ, *see* ċuaiḋ.

cia, *int. pron.*, who, **which**.

ciannor, } *int. adv.*, how, in what **manner**; cia an nóṫ
cionnor, } what is the way? [cinḋaṫ a eccoṫc, what kind is his appearance? *par.* 26.]

Ciappaiġe, *see* Ciappuiḃe.

Ciappuiḃe, *p. n. f.*, Kerry; *see note on par.* 35.

ciḋ, *and* cíḋ, *for* cia; *also for* ġiḋ, *q. v.*: ciḋ tráċt, however, *see par.* 16, *and note.*

cin co, *for* ġion ġo; *see* ġion, ġo *and* co; *see note on par.* 38

cinḋ, *for* cinn, *see* ceann.

cinḋaṫ *for* ciannor, *q. v.*

cinn, *gen., see* ceann.

clann, *n. f., gen.* clainne, *dat.*, clainn, *pl.* clanna, children, clann, family; clanna Móṗna, clanna baoiṫcne, the clanns descended from Morna, and from Baoiscne: clanna Mileḋ, the Milesians.

clanna *and* clanḋa, *see* clann.

cleite, *n. m., gen. id., pl.*, -tiḃe, a feather, or rather a quill; a plume.

cleitiḃe, *see* cleite.

clú, *or* cliu, *n. m., gen. id.*, fame, renown; a ġ-clú, in fame.

clúḋaṁail, *adj.* famous, *see* clúmar.

cluiċe, *n. m., gen. id., pl.* cluiċċe, a game; leaṫ cluiċe, a half-game.

cluiche *or* cluichi, *see* cluiċe.

cluiċċe, *see* cluiċe.

clúmar, *adj., gen. m.* -aip, *fem. and comp.* -aipe, famous.

Cnuċa, *p. n.*, *Cnucha, see note c. on par.* 2.

co, *for* ġo, that, to, till; *also equivalent to* le, with, *q. v.* See cin co, aine, *and note a. on par.* 6; co nor, *see* nor, co m-bi, co m-ba, till was; co n-ḋeṫna, till was made; co torċuiṫ, till was slain; con, *id., see* conacan: co *for* coṁ *or* ċo, as, so, *q. v.*

coḋail, *v. n., inf.*, -laḋ, sleep.

coḋlaḋ, *n. m., gen.*, coḋalta, sleep; na ċoḋlaḋ, in his sleep; am' ċoḋlaḋ, in my sleep, &c., (asleep); *Idioms.*

coḋlaḋ, *see* coḋlaḋ.

Coḋna, *p. n. m., Codna*, a man's name.

Coḋnai, *see* Coḋna.

coġaḋ, *n. m., gen.* -aiḋ, *pl. id. and* coġṫa, war.

coġaḋ, *see* coġaḋ.

**coibċe,** } *obs. n.* dowry. See O Donovan's supplement to
**coibche,** } O'Reilly's Dictionary, *in voce.*
**coill,** *n. f., gen.* coille, *pl.* coillte, *gen. pl.* coillteaḋ, a wood; coill craobać, a branching wood; bóṙo coillteaḋ craob, the border of woods of branches, (*branching*); Welsh *coed*, **see note c. par. 5.**
coille, *gen., see* coill.
coillteaḋ, *gen. pl., see* coill.
**cóiṁoeaċt,** } *n.f.,* attendance, company, escort; a ġ-
**ṡóiṁoeaċt,** } cóiṁoeaċt le, in company with, together
**cóiṁéaoaċt,** } with; **see** *note a. on par.* 14.
**coiṁeta,** *see* cóiṁeuo.
**cóiṁeuo** { *n. m., gen., -oa,* keeping; ꝼean cóiṁeuoa
**cóiṁéao** { (*cpd. noun*), the keeper, man of keeping; *see*
{ ꝼean, *and note a. on par.* 5.
**cóiṁeuoa,** *see* cóiṁeuo.
**cóiṁċionol,** *n. m., gen.* -oil, a meeting, an assembly.
**Coipppe,** *see* Caipbpe.
**com,** *for* coṁ *and* ċum, *q. v.*; com luo, ċum luo, to play.
**coṁ** } *adv.,* **so,** as; equal **to**; *prefix corresponding to* con,
**ċoṁ** { with *or* together. *In comparison, is used with* le
**ċo,** } *and* a'ꞃ (for aguꞃ); *as* coṁ miliꞃ **le** mil, **as sweet as honey;** cá eolaꞃ aġam com maiṫ a'ꞃ tá aġat, I know as well as you do; cá ꞃiao coṁ áꞃo, they are equally high. (*Idioms.*)
**comao,** *i.e.,* co m-baḋ, ġo m-baḋ, till should be.
**comimain,** *for* ċum iomáin, *see* com *and* iomáin.
**cóṁlann** *n. m., gen.,* -ainn; (1), a combat; (2) match, complement; (3) a colleague: beiꞃio cóṁlann, they engage: ꝼean cóṁlainn caoġaio, a man a match for fifty men.
**comlonn,** *for* cóṁlann, *q. v.*
**comluo,** *see under* com.
**cóṁpac,** *n. m., gen.* -ṗaic, a conflict, a **duel**; *properly* **cóṁ-bpac,** *from* cóṁ *and* bpac, the arm.
**comtinol,** *for* cóiṁċionol, *q. v.*
**con,** *for* co *or* com, till; *see* co *and* ġo.
**conacap,** *from* con *and* ꝼaic, *obs. form for* ġo b-ꝼacaoap, till they saw, *q. v. and* co.
**conao,** conio, *obs.,* so it is; conao aꞃ ꞃin, *par.* 29.
**concaoap,** *v. irr.,* 3*rd pers. pl. past tense* (*of* ꝼeicim), they saw; *see* ċonnaipc.
**Concinn,** *see* Cunéinn, *gen. and* Cuċeann, *nom.*
**conio** } *obs. form of* co *and* iꞃ, that it is, so it is; *see* conao
**conic,** } *and note c, on paragraph* 5.

Connaċt, *n. f., Connacht;* see *note on par.* 48; a ʒ-Connaċtaib *or* a ʒ-Connaċt, in Connacht.
Connaċtaib, *dat. pl., see* Connaċt.
ċonnaıṁc, *v. irr.*, 3rd *pers. sing. past tense (of* ḟeıcım), saw; *See* O'Donovan's Grammar, p. 222.
conṫuıcci, *obs. form of the verb* tıʒ, comes; maḋ conṫuıcci, *i.e.,* má tıʒ ɼe *or* má tıocɼaḋ ɼe, if he should come.
Conṫuınn, *see* Cúl-conṫuınn.
Conṫunḋ, *see* Conṫuınn *and* Cúl-conṫuınn,
coɲ, *for* ʒuɲ *or* ʒoɲ; *see* ʒuɲ, ʒo, co, *and* ɲo.
coɼċa, *n. f.,* a district, *as* Corca Oiche, Corca Ui Dhuibhne.
coɼco, *see* coɼċa.
Coɼɲ, *p. n. m., Corr,* a man's name; *see* Luʒaıḋ.
coɲɲ, *adj.* round, *also* odd; coɲɲ-bolʒ, a round bag.
coɲɲ-bolʒ, *from* coɲɲ *and* bolʒ, *q.v.*; a round bag or purse; *compare* cıoɲ-bolʒ *and* ɼeaɲ-bolʒ, *in* O'Donovan's Supplement to Dictionary.
coċuıʒeaḋ, *v. a., past tense, passive voice,* was reared, fed.
cɼaıb, *for* cɼaob, *q. v.*
cɼaob, *n. f., gen.* -oıbe, *pl.* -oba, *gen pl.* cɼaob, a branch, a bough, *see under* coıll.
Cɼımall, *p. n. m., gen.* -aıll, *Crimall,* a man's name; Cumhall's brother.
Cɼot, *p. n. m., pl.* cɼota, *dat.* cɼotaıb, *Sliabh g-crot; see note b. on par* 20.
Cɼottaıb, *see* Cɼot.
cɼuaıḋ, *adj., comp.* cɼuaıḋe, hard; ʒo cɼuaıḋ, strongly.
cɼuaıḋ, *for* cɼuaıḋ, *q. v.*
Cɼuıtne, *for* Cɼuıtne, *q. v.*
Cɼuıtne, *p. n. f., Cruithne,* a woman's name.
cuaċ, *n. f., gen.* cuaıċe, *pl.* cuaċa; also *n. m., gen. and pl.* cuaıċ, (1) a cuckoo, (2) a cup, (3) a curl.
cuaıċ, *see* cuaċ.
ċuaıḋ, *v. irr. past tense (of* teıḋım), went; ċuaıḋ-ɼıom, *for* ċuaıḋ ɼeıɼean, he went.
ċuaıḋ-ɼıom, *see* ċuaıḋ.
cualaıḋ, *for* ċualaıḋ, *q. v.*
ċualaıḋ, *v. ac. irr. past tense (of* cluınım), heard ; ċualamaɼ, we heard (ne emphatic).
ċualamaɼ, *see under* ċualaıḋ.
cualamuɲne, *for* ċualamaɼ-ne, *see* ċualaıḋ.
Cuanaċ, *gen., p. n. m., Cuana,* a man's name; *ua g-Cuanach,* of the O'Cuanas. *See note on par.* 37.
cuca, *see* ċuca.
cuccu, *for* ċuca, *q. v.*

cuccu, *for* cuca, *q. v.*
Cuceann, *p. n. m., gen.* Cuncinn *or* Concinn, *Cucheann,* a man's name, *i.e.* hound-headed.
cucht, *obs. n.* colour ; *see note b, par.* 56.
cucum *for* cugam, *q. v.*
cugam, *pr. pron.,* unto or towards me.
cuice, *for* cuige, *q. v.*
cuid, *n. f., gen. id. and* coda, a portion.
cuige, *pr. pron.* unto him, *from* co *and* é.
cuil, *n. f., gen.* cuile, a corner ; *often used in names of places;* Cuil-contuinn, *Cuil-contuinn, see note e par.* 1.
Cuile contuinn, *see* cuil *and* contuinn.
Cuilleann, *p. n. m., Cuilleann,* name of place, *see* Cuanach, *and note, par.* 37.
Cuillind, *for* Cuilleann, *q. v.*
Cuip, *v. ac., inf.* cup, (1) put, (2) send, (3) wage, (4) plant; cuipicheap, *for* cuipceap, *pass.,* is put ; cuipear, *past ac.* I put ; cuipeadap, they put ; cuipeap, *hist. pres. tense,* puts, &c. ; cuip cuige, send forward to him, cuip a n-eagap, put in form, regulate ; cuip a g-car, suppose ; cuip pointe, determine ; cuip aip ac-la, postpone (*Idioms*).
cuipeadap, *see under* cuip.
cuipear, *see under* cuip.
cuipicheap, *for* cuipceap, *see under* cuip.
Cuipp, *gen. p. n. m., see* Copp.
cuipceap, *see under* cuip.
cul, *n. m., gen.* cuil, (1) the back of anything ; cul cinn, the poll : cul baine, something in reserve, as in a game : (2), a guard, a reserve : pear cuil, a man at one's back as a defence ; aip g-cul, backwards ; pa cul, at the back, (*Idioms*).
cum *for* cum, *q. v.*
cum *or* do cum, *cpd. prep.,* towards, unto, in order that.
cuma, *n.m.,* form, shape, stature ; a cuma, [a eccorg] his appearance : ip cuma liom, it is equal to me.
cum, *v. ac., inf.*-mad, form, devise, shape ; cumam' cpoinic do clainn Neill, let us make a chronicle for the O'Neills.
cumact, *n. f., gen.*-cta, power.
cumactachi, *v. obs.* ye can : *see* cumact, *and par.* 26.
Cumaill, *gen. p. n. m. See* Cumall.
Cumall, *for* Cumall, *q. v.*
Cumall, *p. n. m., gen.*-aill, *Cumhall,* a man's name ; Fionn's father, slain at Cnucha. *See page* 55.

cumtá, *partic. adj.* (*from* cum), formed, shaped: veag-cumtá, well-shaped, shapely.
Cumuill, *for* Cúmaill; *see* Cúmall.
cuncinn, *gen.* of cuceann, *q. v.*
cup, *for* gup; *see* gup, go, co *and* po.
cupab, *for* gup ab, that it was : so it was.
cuy, *for* gup: *see* go and gup.
v', *for* vo and ve.
vá, *num. adj.* two ; used when the noun is expressed.
vá, *conj.* if: vá m-bav, if should be.
v'a (*from* ve *and* a), of his, her, its, their; *obs.*
v'a (*from* vo *and* a), to his, her, its, their.
v'a (*from* vo *and* a *rel.*), of *or* to which *or* what.
Vaipe, *p. n. m. Daire*, a man's name.
vam, *pr. pron.* to me, by me; from vo and me.
van, *expletive*, then, indeed, just, &c. *See note a, par.* 4.
vána, *adj. indec.* bold, brave.
vap, *prep.* by; vap liom, methinks; vap leat, it seems to thee, (*Idioms*): vap an láim pin, by that hand; *see note a, par.* 34, and O'Donovan's Gram., p. 299.
vat, *n. m., gen.* vatá, *pl.* vatanna, a color.
ve, *prep.* of, off, from : lean ve, follow on, persevere.
vé, *pr. pron.* of, off, or from him *or* it: ve pin, of that, whence: ve, *par.* 11, in consequence of that.
veabtha, *obs. n. gen., see* veabav.
veabav, *obs. n.* a dispute : *See note c, par.* 1.
veacaiv, *v. irr. subj. past* (of teiv) went ; go n-veacaiv pe, till he went.
veag, *indec.*, good : (*comes before the noun.*)
veag-cumtá, *adj.* well-shaped. *See* cumtá.
vean, *for* vian, *q. v.*
veapbpátaip, *n. m., gen.*-éap, *pl.*-páitpe, *or* -páitpeaca, a brother: a real brother; veapbpátaip a atap, his father's brother, his uncle.
veapg, *adj., gen. m.* veipg, *f.* veipge ; *comp.* veipge, red, bright red; Vaipe veapg, Daire (the) red.
veapna, *for* veápnav, *q. v.*
veápnav, *v. irr., subj. past* passive of veun ; go n-veápnav, till was made ; v'a n-veápnav, of what was made.
veap, *adj.* (1) south, (2) right, (3) pretty ; bu veap, *for* ó veap, southward; a n-veap, from the south, *i.e.* ó an veap; veap-láim, the right hand.
vechaiv, *for* veacaiv, *q. v.*
vegaiv, *for* viaig, *q. v.*
veimin, *adj.* certain, sure ; go veimin, indeed.

Ueimne, *p. n. m. Deimne*, a name of Fionn.
ueimniuġaḋ, *n. m. gen.*, -miġṫe, testing, proving.
ueip, *v. ac. irr.* say; ueip pe, says he; *imp.* abaip; *past*, ḋuḃaipc, *inf.* do pað.
ueipe, *or* ueipeaḋ, *n. m.* the end: ɣo ueipe, **to the end.**
ueipɣ, *adj. gen. m.*; *see* ueapɣ.
ueipɣi, *for* ueipɣ *or* ueipɣe. *See* ueapɣ.
ueipide *for* de pin *or* de; *see under* de.
ueiċḃip, *obs. n.* (1), reason, occasion; (2), difference; *see par.* 14 *and note c on par.* **1.**
ueiṫḃip, *for* ueiċḃip, *q. v.*
Uemne, *for* Ueimne, *q. v.*
de'n, *prep. and art.* de *and* an, **of the.**
uéna, *for* deun, *q. v.*
ueo } *n. f. obs.* an end, the last; ɣo ueo, **for ever;** fá
ueoiɣ } ḃeoiɣ, finally, at last.
ueoiɣ *for* ueoiɣ, *or* ueo, *q. v.*
ueop, *n. m., gen.* ueoip; *pl.* ueopa, tears.
uépa *for* ueopa; *see* ueop.
uepna *for* ueápnaḋ, *q. v.*
uep *for* ueap, *q. v.*
ueun, *v. ac. irr.* make, do; *inf.* ueunaḋ; *see* ɣniḋ.
ueunaḋ, *inf.* of ueun, to make, *q. v.*
di, *pr. pron.* **of, off, for, from,** *or* **to her.**
di *for* dá, two, *q. v.*
di *for* d'a, to his, to which, &c., *q. v.*
dia *for* d'a; *see* dia *and* d'a.
dia *for* dá, if, *q. v.*
diaiɣ, *n. f. obs.* **rear,** wake, end; 'na ḃiaiɣ pin, after that; diaiɣ a n-diaiɣ, diaiɣ ap aile, after each other; a n-diaiɣ a ċinn, after his head, *i.e.*, headlong. (*Idioms.*)
dian, *adj., comp.* déine, violent, **eager,** vehement.
diana *for* d'a n-a, &c.
diḃ, *pr. pron.*, of, off, *or* from ye; also for díoḃ, *q. v*; diḃpide *for* diḃ-pide *or* diḃ-pe, *emphatic form.*
diḃpide, *emph. pron. obs; see under* diḃ.
diċeadal, } *n. obs.* a kind of incantation; *see* paragraph 54,
diceoul, } and note on same, p. 67.
dim, *obs.* form of díom, off me, *or* dam, to me; dim-pa, *emphatic*; cic dim, *now* ciɣ liom, comes with me, I can.
dimḃaḋa, *obs. v.* to swim; from do to, im *or* iom, *particle* (*see note on par.* 28) and báiḋ, **immerse.**
dim-pa, *emph.*; *see* dim.
din, *expletive*; *see* dan, *and note a on par.* 4.

**díob,** *pr. pron.* of, off, *or* from them; **díob-ṡan,** *emph.*: **díob ṡo** of these, **díob ṡúd,** of those yonder; **naonḃaṙ díob,** nine of them.

**dírċiṡ** *adj.*, nimble, fierce; *see* **imdiċṙciṙ.**

**dirgell,** *obs. n.* fright, consternation; *possibly same as* **ṙgeimle,** surprise; **di** *is here an intensitive particle*: **dirgell ṙceill.** sudden fright (**ṙgill,** quick, O'Reilly), *see note e. par.* 56.

**díṫṙeaḃ,** *n. m.* a retreat, a cell for a hermit; **díṫṙeaḃ coille,** a hermitage in the forest.

**diṫṙeiḃ** *for* **díṫṙeaḃ,** *q. v.*

**diu,** *obs. n.* a day; *used in* **a n-diu** *or* **i n-diu** (*or* **a n-iuḋ**), to-day, now; *also* **di** *or* **dia,** *as in* **dia luain.** &c.

**dna,** *obs. for* **dan,** *q. v.*

**do,** *or* **no,** *q. v., par. prefixed to past tense, ac. and pass.*

**do,** *prep.* to, for, by; *also sometimes for* **de.**

**do** *or* **a,** *par., prefixed to infinitive mood.*

**do,** *par. prefixed to conditional mood, ac. and pass.,* **and *some-times in other cases*;** *see* **aṫ.**

**do** (*for* **a**), *rel. pron.*, who, which, that.

**do,** *poss. pron.*, thy.

**do,** *num.* two, *used without the noun, as* **ṙin é an dó,** that is (the) two; *see* **dá.**

**dó,** *pr. pron.*, to him, by, *or* for him.

**doḃ,** *for* **do buḋ,** *asser. v.*, it was; *see* **buḋ.**

**dóiḃ** *for* **dóiḃ,** *q. v.*

**dóiḃ,** *pr. pron.* to them, for, *or* by them.

**doiṙḃ,** *adj., comp.* **doiṙbe** morose, ill-natured.

**do'n** *prep. and art.*, **de** and **an,** to, for, or by the.

**draoi,** *n. m.*, a druid, a magician; **ban-draoi,** a druidess.

**dream,** *n. m.*, a company, people; **dream de'n t-ṙean-ḟéinn,** a company of the old Fiann.

**dṙem,** *for* **dream,** *q. v.*

**duḃaiṙṫ,** *v. irr. past tense of* **deiṙ,** said; *see* **deiṙ.**

**dúin,** *gen. of* **dún,** *q. v.*

**duine,** *n. m.*, *gen. id., pl.* **daoine,** *gen.* **-eaḋ,** a man, a person, male or female, anyone; **ṙean-duine,** an old man or woman; *pl.* people; *see note on par.* 31.

**dúine** *for* **dúin;** *see* **dún.**

**duiṫ,** *pr. pron.* to thee; **duiṫ-ṙe.** *emphatic.*

**duiṫ-ṙe,** *emph. pron.*; *see* **duiṫ.**

**dul,** *v. irr., inf. of* **ṫeid,** to go, going.

**dún,** *n. m.*, *gen. and pl.* **dúin** (*obs.* **dúine** *and* **dúnaid**), a fortress, a fort; **ṙeaṙ an dúin,** the master of the fortress; **ṙaiṫċe an dúin,** the lawn of the castle.

dúnaid *for* dúin, *see* dún.
é, *pers. pron.* he, him, it; ıſ é, it is he.
eać, *n. m., gen. and pl.* eić, a steed, a horse.
Eaċaċ, *p. n. m., gen. of* Eaċaıḋ, *q. v.*
Eaċaıḋ, } *p. n. m., gen.* Eaċaċ, *Eochaidh*, a man's name, a horseman; mac Eaċaċ Ḟınn, son of fair Eochaidh; Loċ n-Eaċaċ, *or* n-Eaċaċ, Eochaidh's lake, Lough Neagh. Latinized *Achaius*.
Eoċaıḋ, }
eaḋ, *pers. pron.* he, it; *form of* é; ıſ eaḋ, 'ſeaḋ, it is, yes; ní h-eaḋ, it is not, nay, no.
eaḋon, *adv. videlicet*, namely, that is to say, 'ſe ſın le ſáḋ: abbreviated form .ı., *i.e.* Also written ıoḋon.
eaḋoṗṗa, *pr. pron.* between them, from ıoıſ.
eaġal, } *n. f., and* eaġaıl; *gen.* eaġla, fear, timidity; buḋ eaġal léı, it was a fear with her; tá eaġla oſm, I am afraid. (*Idiom*.)
eaġla, }
ealta, *n. m.* a flock, a herd, a drove, a troop.
Eaſnánaıḋ, *obs. p. n. dat. pl. Earnain*, name of certain districts; *see paragraph* 2 *and note a on same*.
eatuſſa *for* eaḋoṗṗa, *q. v.*
ecaıl. *for* eaġaıl, *or* eaġal, *q. v.*
eccoſc, *obs. n. m.* appearance; *see under* cuma.
eċaıḋ, *for* Eaċaıḋ *or* Eoċaıḋ, *q. v.*
eıc, *n. m. pl. of* eaċ, *q. v.*
éıcſı *for* éıġſe, *q. v.*
éıḋe, *n. m.* armour, accoutrement.
eıḋıṙḋealuıġeaſ, *v. ac. rel. pres. tense*, which distinguish.
éıġean, *n. m., gen.*-ġın, necessity, force; ḋo ḃí éıġean, there was necessity; ıſéıġean lıom ſáḋ, I must say.
éıġın, *adj.* necessary; ḋoḃ' éıġın ḋam, it was necessary for me.
éıġſe, *n. f., gen. id.*, literature, learning.
eıle, *ind. adj. pron.* other, another; *see note on par*. 3.
éıneaċ, *n. m. gen.*-nıġ, protection, countenance; aıſ m' éıneaċ-ſa, under my safeguard.
Eıſe, *p. n. f., gen.*-ſeann, *dat.*-ſınn, *Eire*, Ireland; *see* ċeana.
Eıſeann, *p. n. f. gen.*; *see* Eıſe.
Eıſenḋ *for* Eıſeann; *see* Eıſe.
eıſġ *for* eıſıġ, *q. v.*
eıſġeaḋaſ; *see under* eıſıġ.
eıſıḋ *for* eıſıġ, *q. v.*
eıſıġ. *v. n. and ac., inf.* eıſıġe, (1) rise, (2) go, (3) happen; ná h-eıſıġ, go not; eıſıġ uaınn, go from us; eıſıġ amaċ, rise out.

Éiṙinn, *p. n. f. dat.*, *see* Eipe.
éiṙeaṅ, *pers. pron. emph.*, he, he himself.
eite, *n. m. or f. pl.*, eiteaḋa *or* eitiḋe, a wing, a pinion.
én, *for* aon, one, *q. v.*
eneċ, *for* éineaċ, *q. v.*
eo, *or* iaċ, *obs. n. m.*, *gen. id.*, a salmon; *see* braḋán.
Eoċaiḋ, *see under* Eaċaiḋ.
Eoċamán, *p. n. m.*, *gen.*, áin, *Eochaman*, a man's name.
Eochamáin, *p. n. m. gen.*, *see* Eoċamán.
erḃaḋ, *obs. v.* was assigned, was appointed.
Erinn, *for* Eirinn, *q. v.*
Ernaiḃ, *for* Eaṡnánaiḃ, *q. v.*
eriḋe *for* eireaṅ; *see* é *and* éireaṅ.
erium *for* éireaṅ *see* é, eriḋe *and* éireaṅ.
eteḋa *for* eiteaḋa; *see under* eite.
fá *for* buḋ *or* ba, *q. v.*

fá,
faoi,
{ *prep.* (1) under, (2) for, (3) at, (4) towards; fá'n loċ, under, or in the lake; creaḋ fá, what for, why? fá ḋeoiġ, at last; fá'n am rin, at that time; fá tuairim, towards. (*Idioms*), [luiḋ fai, went towards her.]

facaiḋ, *v. irr. past subj.*, saw; go b-facaiḋ re, till he saw; gob-facaḋar, till they saw; *from* feicim, I see.
facaḋar, *v. irr.*, they saw; *see under* facaiḋ.
fácċḃáḋ *for* fáġḃaḋ; *see under* fáġ.
fácċlail *for* fáġḃail; *see under* fáġ.
facca *for* fáġḃail, *see under* fáġ.
facca, *for* facaiḋ, *q. v.*, *and* acca.
faccaiḋ *for* facaiḋ, *q. v.*
faḋa *adj. comp. irr.* faiḋe *or* fia, long, distant.
faeḃur *for* faoḃar, *q. v.*
fáġ, *v. ac., inf.* fáġḃáil, leave, quit; ḋ'fáġ, left (past); gur fáġ re, that he left; mac ḋ'fáġḃáil ḋo, a son to be left by him, that he left a son; ḋá b-fáġḃaḋ (*cond.*), if had left.
cáġaiḃ *for* fáġ *or* ḋ'fáġ; *see* accaiḃ *and* fáġ.
fáġḃaḋ., *cond.*; *see under* fáġ.
fáġḃáil, *inf.*; *see under* fáġ.
fageiḃ *or* fogeiḃ, *obs.* find; *see* fogáiḃ.
fai *for* faoi, *or* fuiċi; *see under* fá.
faiche, *for* faitċe, *q. v.*
faiḋir *for* fuiḋir, *q. v.*
fáil, *obs. n. m. gen.*, of destiny; inir fáil, Ireland.
failliġeḋ, *for* foillriġċi, *q. v.*
fáilteaċ, *adj.* welcome, agreeable.

ꞃᴀıꞃ, *prep., for* ᴀıꞃ, on, *q. v.*
ꞃáıꞃᵹıḃ, *v. ac. pres. 3rd pers. sing.*, presses.
ᴀıċċe, *n. f.* a green, a field, a lawn; ꞃᴀıċċe ᴀn ḋúın, the exercise-green of the fortress.
ꞃᴀn *or* ꞃá'n, *prep. and art.* ꞃá *and* ᴀn, under the.
ꞃᴀn, *v. ac., inf.* ꞃᴀnᴀċᴛ *and* ꞃᴀnᴀṁᴀın, stay, remain; ꞃᴀnᴀıḋ, *3rd pers.* tarries; ᴅ'ꞃᴀn ḃeo, who remained alive; ꞃᴀn ᵹo ꞃóıl, wait awhile; ꞃᴀn ᵹo ꞃocᴀıꞃ, stay quiet.
ꞃᴀnᴀıḋ, *see under* ꞃᴀn.
ꞃᴀnn, *adj., comp.* ꞃᴀınne, weak, infirm, languid.
ꞃᴀoḃᴀꞃ, *n. m., gen.* -ᴀıꞃ, an edge; ꞃᴀoḃᴀꞃ-ċꞃuᴀıḋ, *adj.* of the hard (edged) weapons; *compare* ꞃᴀoḃᴀꞃ-ᵹlᴀꞃ.
ꞃᴀoḃᴀꞃ-ċꞃuᴀıḋ, *cpd. adj., see under* ꞃᴀoḃᴀꞃ.
ꞃᴀoı, *prep., see* ꞃá, under, for; ꞃᴀoı ᴀn ᴛ-ꞃáṁᴀıl ꞃın, in that way.
ꞃᴀꞃcᴀıḃ *for* ꞃáᵹᴀıḃ *and* ᴅ'ꞃáᵹ; *see* ꞃáᵹ, *also* O'Don. Gram., *p.* 258, *and* ꞃáꞃᵹᴀıḃ *in* Supp. to Dictionary.
ꞃᴀꞃꞃᴀḋ, *n. m.* company, people; *see note* 3, *p.* 56; 'nᴀ ḃ-ꞃᴀꞃꞃᴀḋ, among them, belonging to them; ᴀ ḃ-ꞃᴀꞃꞃᴀḋ, with, or on the side of (*compound prep.*).
ꞃᴀꞃꞃᴀᴅ *for* ꞃᴀꞃꞃᴀḋ, *q. v.*
ꞃᴀꞃꞃᴀıᴅ *for* ꞃᴀꞃꞃᴀḋ, *q. v.*
ꞃáꞃᴀċ, *n. m., gen.* -ᴀıᵹ, *pl.* -ᴀıᵹe, *dat. pl.* -ᴀċᴀıḃ *and* -ᴀıᵹıḃ, a wild, a desert; *see* ꞃoꞃᴀoıꞃ *and* ꞃáꞃuıᵹ.
ꞃᴀꞃᴀch *for* ꞃáꞃᴀċ, *q. v.*
ꞃᴀꞃᴀıᴅ *for* ᴅ'ꞃáꞃuıᵹ; *see* ꞃáꞃuıᵹ.
ꞃáꞃᴀıᵹe, *pl. of* ꞃáꞃᴀċ, *q. v.*
ꞃᴀꞃᴛᴀıᴅ, *see* ᴀꞃᴛᴀıᴅ, ꞃᴀꞃᴛuıᵹıḃ, *and* ꞃᴀꞃᴛuıᵹ.
ꞃᴀꞃᴛuᴅ, *see* ᴀꞃᴛuḋ, ꞃᴀꞃᴛuᵹᴀḋ, *and* ꞃᴀꞃᴛuıᵹ.
ꞃᴀꞃᴛuᵹᴀḋ, *inf., see under* ꞃᴀꞃᴛuıᵹ.
ꞃᴀꞃᴛuıᵹ, *v. ac.* retain, fasten; ᴅ'ꞃᴀꞃᴛuᵹᴀḋ ᴀᵹᴀınn, to secure with us; ꞃᴀꞃᴛuıᵹıḃ, *3rd pers. pres. ind.* seizes: *also*, agree to. See *note on par.* 31.
ꞃᴀꞃᴛuıᵹıḃ, *ind. pres. 3rd pers.; see under* ꞃᴀꞃᴛuıᵹ.
ꞃáꞃuıᵹ, *v. ac., inf.* -uᵹᴀḋ, lay waste, devastate; ᴅ'ꞃáꞃuıᵹ, wasted; *from* ꞃáꞃ, empty, *obs.; see* ꞃáꞃᴀċ.
ꞃáċ, *n. m., gen. id., and* ꞃáċᴀ, cause, reason.
ꞃeᴀċᴛ, *obs. n. f.*, time, turn; ᵹᴀċ ꞃe ꞃeᴀċᴛ, every second turn; ꞃeᴀċᴛ n-ᴀnn, once upon a time; ᴀ n-éınꞃeᴀċᴛ *or* ᴀ n-ᴀoınꞃeᴀċᴛ le, together with; *see note on par.* 30.
ꞃeᴀḋᴀ, *gen. of* ꞃıoḋ, a wood; *see* ᴍáᵹ ꞃeᴀḋᴀ.
ꞃeᴀᴅᴀꞃ *or* ꞃıᴅıꞃ, *def. v.* know; ní ꞃeᴀᴅᴀꞃ me, I know not.
ꞃeᴀꞃ, *n. m., gen. and pl.* ꞃıꞃ, *gen. pl.* ꞃeᴀꞃ, a man; ꞃeᴀꞃ nᴀ ꞃeoᴅ, the owner of the jewels; *see also* cóıṁeᴅ *and* ᴅún; ꞃeᴀꞃ ꞃáıl (of the) men of Inisfail.

feaṅgaċ *adj., comp.* -aiġe, angry, wrathful.
fearoa, *adv.* henceforth.
feċt *for* feaċt, *q. v.*
feic, *gen., see* linn feic.
féin, *emph. pron.* own, self; a ḟeoio féin, his own valuables; ⁊inn féin, ourselves; linn féin, by ourselves.
feinio *for* fiann, *q. v.*
féinniḋe, *n. m.* a warrior, champion, hero, soldier; an oá bain-ḟéinniḋe, the two heroines.
fen *for* fean, *q. v.*
fenait, *for* beinio *q. v.* and beinim; feapaim, I give, (O'R.)
feṅgaċ, *for* feaṅgaċ, *q. v.*
feroa *or* ferta; *for* feanoa, *q. v.*
fet *or* feo, *def. v.* relates; *see* at fet.
fetan *for* feaoan, *q. v.*
feuoaim, *v. def.* I can; feuoamuio, we can (*pl.*); feuoaim má'r áil liom, I can if I choose.
feuoamuio, we can: *see* feuoaim.
Fiacail, *p. n. m., Fiacail*, a man's name, son of Cucheann.
fiaccail *for* fiacail *and* fiagail, *q. v.*
Fiagail, *p. n. m., gen.* fiagla, *Fiagail*, a man's name, son of Codna.
fiagla, *gen.* of fiagail, *q. v.*
fianaigeaċt *for* fiannuiġeaċt, *q. v.*
fianboich, *for* fiann-boċ, *q. v.*
fianboichi *for* fiann-boiċe, *gen.; see* fiann-boċ.
Fiann, *coll. n. f., gen.* féinne, *dat.* féinn, the Fiann; the soldiers of Fionn collectively: one of the Fiann; *pl.* féinne and fianna; the Fianna Eireann: *see pp.* 54, 75, &c. Opeam oe'n t-rean-ḟéinn, a company of the old Feinne.
fiann-boiċ, *dat.; see* fiann-boċ.
fiann-boiċe, *gen.; see* fiann-boċ *and* boċ.
fiann-boċ, *cpd. n. f., gen.* -oiċe, *dat.* -oiċ, *pl.* -oċa, a hunting-booth or tent: *see* p. 50, *and* boċ.
Fiannuiġeaċt, *n. f., gen.* -eaċta; the Fiannship: the chief leadership of the Fiann. *See note b*, par. 1. p. 54. Also the customs, adventures, attributes, &c, of the fiann; laoiḋċe fiannuiġeaċta, lays of the Fiann; rgeul fiannuiġeaċta, a story of the Fiann, a romance.
fianur, *n. m. obs.* the headship of the Fiann, the chief command of the armies; fianur fean fáil, the leadership of the men of Ireland; *see* fiannuiġeaċt.

fıȯ or fıoȯ, *n. m.* a wood; fıoȯ ʒaıble, *FiodhGaibhle*, the name of a place. *See note par.* 22, *p.* 59.
fıocellaċt *for* fıṫċeallaċt, *q. v.*
fıl *for* fuıl, *q. v.*
fıleaȯ, ⎫ *n. m., gen.* fılıȯ, *pl. id. and* fıleaȯa, a poet;
fıle, ⎭ *see pars.* 53 *and* 54, *and notes par.* 50, *and* 54.
fıle, fılıȯ, *n. m. gen. See under* fıle.
fılıȯeaċt, ⎫ *n. f., gen.* -eaċta, the art of poetry; poetry;
fıleaċt, ⎭ minstrelsy: le fılıȯeaċt, to study poetry.
fılıȯechṫ, *for* fılıȯeaċt, *q. v.*
fınn, *adj. gen.*, fair; *see* fıonn.
fınn, *p. n. m., gen.*, of Fionn; *see* fıonn.
fınn, *p. n. m., nom. for* fıonn, *q. v.*
fıno, *p. n. m. nom. and acc. for* fıonn, *q. v.*
fınnéıcer, *p. n. m., for* fınnéıʒear, *q. v.*
fınnéıʒear, *p. n. m. Finneigeas*, a man's name; *note, p.* 67.
fınnfaȯ, ⎫ *n. obs.* feathers; *also* fur; *see* fıonnfaȯ *or* fıonnaȯ
fıonnfaȯ, ⎭ *in* O'Reilly's Dict.; *also* fıonnaȯ, depilation.
fıoȯ-ʒaıble, *p. n. m. Fiodhgaibhle*; *see note par.* 22.
fıonn, *p. n. m., gen.* fınn, *Fionn*; a man's name; Fionn, son of Cumhall. *See letter page* 70., *et passim.*
fıonn, *adj. gen. m.* fınn; *f. and comp.* fınne, fair, white, true, fine; fıonn-ȯuıne, a fair man.
fıonnṁáʒ, *p. n. m. Fionnmhagh*; *see note b, par.* 6.
fıop, *adj., comp.* fıpe, true, real; ʒo fıop, truly, indeed, verily; fıop-uırʒe, spring-water.
fır, *gen. and pl. of* fear; *see* fear, a man.
fır *for* fıop, true, *q. v.*
fıor, *n. m., gen.* feara, knowledge, intelligence; ȯ'fıor a mıc, to visit her son; ȯ'a fıor, to his knowing, to get intelligence of him: tá a fıor aʒam, its knowledge is with me, *i. e.* I know; fopar feara aır Eıpınn, an understanding or history of knowledge on Ireland. (*Idioms.*)
fır *for* fıor, *q, v.*; *also* a vision.
fıṫċeallaċt, *n. f.* chess playing, the art of playing chess; *compare* ıarʒaıpeaċt, fılıȯeaċt, realʒaıpeaċt.
fláıṫ, *n. m., gen. id. and* fláṫa, *pl.* fláṫa *and* fláıṫe, a prince, a chief; fláıṫ-ʒoba, a chief-smith, the head of his craft; *see note on pars.* 37 *and* 42 *a.* flaıtear, princedom, reign; flaıteaṁa, heaven, the kingdom; cóṁ-flaıtear, a joint reign; flaıteaṁaıl, princely, generous; *used adjectively in composition.*
fláıṫ-ʒoba, *cpd. n. m.* a chief-smith; *see* fláıṫ.
fláıṫ-ʒobann *for* fláıṫ-ʒoba, *q. v. also* fláıṫ *and* ʒoba.

fó, *prep.* under, for, at about; *see* fá *or* faoi.
fo, *obs. par. for* do *or* po, *q. v.*
foceipurim, *obs.; i.e.* po cuirre, he put or aimed; *see par.* 41.; fo-cepd, he put; *see* O'Don. Supp.
focen, fócen, *obs.; i. e.* fáilteac, welcome. *See* O'Don.
foda *for* fada, long, *q. v.*
fogeib, *obs. v.* found, got; *i. e.* do ġeib *or* fuair, *3rd pers. past. ind. of* irr. *v.* ġeibim, I find; *see* foġeban, he could find: **O'Donovan**, Supp.
foglaid *for* fóglaide, *q. v.*
fóglaide, *n. m., gen. id. pl.* -aidce, a robber, a plunderer.
foglaim *for* fógluim, *q. v.*
fógluim, *v. ac., inf. id.* learn; d'fógluim, to learn *or* (he) learned; fóiġleomad, *fut.*, I will learn.
fogluim rium *for* d'fógluim re, he learned; *see* fógluim.
foiob, ) *obs. n.* arms, armour, accoutrements, *spolia:* *see*
foḃḃ, ) eide, *and note c, par.* 5.
foillrigci, *v. ac. hab. past.* (from foillriġ), used to be made manifest or shown.
foicrib, *n. obs., dat. of* foicpe, woods, wilds; *compare* foircbe, *vastatio*, in O'Donovan's Supp. *See* fárac.
fola, *gen.; see* fuil.
folc, *n. m., gen.* foilc, hair: *now generally* a head of hair; folc fraoic, the tops of the heath.
foluiġid, *v. ac.* 3rd *pers. pl. ind. pres. (from* foluiġ) they cover or hide; *inf.* folac *and* foluġad; dul a b-folac, to go ahide.
fó'n, *prep. and art.*; fó *and* an, **under the.**
fop, *obs. intens. par.* very; *for* up, *q. v.*
for,
forr, { *obs. form of* air, on, upon, *q. v.,* (r *added before a vowel*;) forr a m-bí, on which is (usually); for ci *for* air ci, *see* ci.
forbad, *v. obs.* was reared, grew up; *compare* O'Reilly, forbair, grow thou; *and* O'Don. Supp., forbair, *glisco, and* forbairc .1. bireac, increase.
forar,
foraor, { *n. m., gen.* -air *and* aoir; *n. f.* foraoir, *gen.* -aoire; *pl.* -ire *and* -reaca, a forest, a haunt
foraiġir, { of wild beasts; foraoir an c-rléibe (*gen.*) of the forest of the mountain.
forbrid, *v. obs.* **flourishes**; *see under* forbad *and* blácuiġ.
for-gnanda *for* ur-gnanda, *q. v., and* for.
forra *or* forra *for* orra, *q. v., also,* air *and* for.
forc *for* orc, *q. v., also,* air *and* for.
fór, *adv.* yet, as yet, still; *conj.* moreover; cuille fór, furthermore; ac fór, yet still.

fṅaich *for* fṅaoiċ; *see* fṅaoċ.
fṅaoċ, *n. m.*, *gen.* fṅaoiċ, heath; *see under* foḷc.
fṅaoiċ, *gen. of* fṅaoċ, *q. v.*
fṅi, *old form of* ne *or* ḷe, with, by, for; fṅi né faḍa, for a long time; *see also* ḷa.
fṅia, *pr. pron.*, *for* nia *or* ḷéi, with her.
fṅiṙ, *pr. pron.*, *for* niṙ *or* ḷeiṙ, with him.
fṅiṙum, *emph. pr. pron. obs.*, *for* niṙ *or* ḷeiṙ-ṙean.
fṅiċ, *v. irr. past tense pass.* was found; *from* fáġ, *see note par.* 52, *and Bourke's Gram.*, *p.* 147.
fṅiċh *for* fṅiċ, *q. v.*
fṅiċhnuṙach, *adj. obs.* morose, fretful; *see* ḍoinḃ, *also* fṅioċnaṙaċ *and* fṅiċneaṙaċ, O'R.
fṅiu-ṙum, *emph. pr. pron. obs. for* niu-ṙan *and* ḷeo-ṙan.
fṅomaḍ, *v. obs.* proving, testing, making trial; *see* ḍeiṁniuġaḍ *and par.* 55.
ṙuaḃaiṙ, *v. obs.* attacks; *see* ṙuaḃaiṙc, an attack, an essay.
ṙuaiṙ, *v. irr. 3rd pers. past ind.* got, found; *see under* fo ġeiḃ.
ṙuaiṙ, *adj. gen. m. and dat. f. of* ṙuaṙ, cold.
ṙuaiṙ-ḃeoiḷ (*see* ùaiṙ-ḃeoiḷ) *adj. obs.* cold, *i.e.* ṙuaṙ.
ṙuaṙ, *adj., comp.* ṙuaiṙe, *gen. m.* ṙuaiṙ, *dat. f. id.*, cold.
ṙuaċ, *n. m.*, *gen.* ṙuaċa, hatred; ṙuaċ buan, lasting enmity.
ṙuiḍiṙ, *v. obs.* marries; *see* póṙaḍ; *note on par.* 37 *and* 42 *a*; *see* ċuaiḍ *and* ḷuiḍ.
**ṙuiḷ**, *f. n.*, *gen.* ṙoḷa, blood; ṙġéiċ ṙoḷa, a shower of blood; ḍeoṙa ṙoḷa, tears of blood.
ṙuiḷech, *adj.* bloody; *see* ṙuiḷceaċ.
ṙuiḷceaċ, *adj.*, *comp.* -ciġe, bloody, blood-shedding.
ṙuine, } *v. inf.* to bake, roast, cook; ḍ'ḟuineaḍ, to roast;
ṙuineaḍ, } iaṙ n-a ḟuineaḍ, after being cooked.
ṙuiṙne, *pr. pron. for* uinṙe, aiṙni, *or* uiṙni, on her, *q. v.*
ṙuiċhiḃ, *pr. pron. for* fúċa, at them, *q. v.*, *and* fá.
ṙuiċhiḃ-ṙum, *emph. pr. pron. obs. for* fúċa-ṙan, *q. v.*
ṙuiċ *for* cuiċ, *q. v.*
fuċ, *p. n. m. Futh*, a man's name.
fúċa, *pr. pron.* under, about, at them; fúċa-ṙan, *emph.*
fúċa-ṙan, *emph. pr. pron.* at them; *see* fúċa.
ġaḃ, *v. ac.*, *inf.* ġaḃáiḷ, (1) take, seize; (2) conceive; (3) go, come, pass; ḍo ġaḃ ṙe, *past tense* (ġaḃ-ṙam), he took; ġaḃaṙ, *hist. pres.*, takes; ġaḃḍaoiṙ (ġaḃḍaíṙ) *conditional*, would take (charge of); ġaḃaṙ ceaḍ ḍe, takes leave of; ġaḃ a ḷeiċ, come aside; aġ ġaḃáiḷ an ḃóċaiṙ, going the road; ġaḃ ṙómaċ, go forward; ġaḃ aḃṙán, sing a song. (*Idioms*.)

gab *for* gáb, *q. v.*
gabar, *hist. pres. tense,* takes; *see under* gab.
gabvair *for* gabvaoir; *q. v. and* gab.
gabvaoir, *cond.* would take; *see under* gab.
gab-ram *for* vo gab re, he took; *see under* gab.
gaċ, *indec. adj. pron.*, each, every; gaċ n-aon, everyone; gaċ uile niḋ. everything; *see* caċ; gaċ ṅe reaċt, *see under* reaċt, *and note on par.* 44.
gaev *or* gaet *for* goin, *q. v.*, *and note c, par.* 5.
gaet, *see* gaev *and* goin.
gaible *for* gaible; *q. v.*, *and* riob-gaible.
gaible, *see* riob-gaible. *and note on par.* 22.
gail, *n. f.*, *gen.* gaile, valour; gail *also gen. of* gal, *q. v.*
gairiv, *3rd pers. pl. pr. ind. of* gair, *q. v.*; *also* goiriv.
gair, *v. ac., inf.* gairim, call, shout, cry; gairiv, they cry or call; gairivir, *hab. past,* they used to call or name; air n-a ngairm, named, termed; *see* goir *and* goiriv; vo gairċi, used to be called.
gairivir, *hab. past tense ac. of* gair, *q. v.*; *also,* goirivir.
gairm, *inf. and part. of* gair, *q. v.*
gairtea *for* gairċi, *q. v.*, goir *and* gair.
gairċi, *hab. past tense, pass; see under* gair.
gairceo *for* gairgiv; *see* gairge.
gairge, *n. f., gen. id. and* -iḋ, valour, bravery, prowess.
gairgiv *for* gairge, *q. v.*
gal, *n. m., gen.* gail, prowess, valour; *also written* gail, *q. v.*; an gail, *gen.*, of the warfare.
galaċ, *adj., gen. m.* -aig, valiant, brave; *from* gal.
galaiv *for* galaiċ, *q. v. and* galaċ.
galaig, *adj. gen.*; *see* galaċ.
gan, *prep.* without; (*see* cen) gan anam, without life.
geall, *n. m., gen. and pl.* gill, (1) a promise, a pledge; (2) a favour, a prize, a wager; (3) regard, desire; mar ġeall air, in regard of, because; reapann a ngeall, mortgaged land; ní'l aon ġeall aige air, he has no regard for it; an t-ain-geall, the great regard. (*Idioms.*)
gearr, *v. ac., inf.* -aḋ, cut; gearr ve, cut off.
geib (ro geib) *past,* found; *see* ġeibim.
geib (ro geib) *obs. past*; *see* ġeibim.
ġeibim, *v. irr.* I find, or get; *same as* ragaim; rogeib *or* rageib, *that is,* vo ġeib *or* rágaib, *obs.* found; ruair, got, found; ruair re amaċ, he discovered.
giv, *conj.* though, although, yet.
giveaḋ, *conj.* yet, nevertheless.

ᵹilla *for* ᵹiolla, *q. v.*
ᵹille *for* ᵹiolla, *q. v.*
ᵹiolla, *n. m.*, *gen. id.*, *pl.* -aiḋe *and* aḋa, an attendant, a
youth, a man-servant, a *gillie*. ᵹiolla aiṁm, an
armour-bearer; ᵹiolla coire, a footman; ᵹiolla
eiċ, a groom; ᵹiolla múċain, a chimney-sweeper;
ᵹiollaḋa an t-ṡluaiᵹ, attendants on an army. O'R.
ᵹion ᵹo; ᵹen ᵹo; cen co, *conj.* although, although not;
see cin co, co *and* ᵹo, *and note on par.* 38. *When
negative, it is made up of* ᵹé, although, ná, not, *and*
ᵹo, that; *when affirmative, it is put simply for* ᵹeḃ
ᵹo *or* ᵹiḃ ᵹo. O'Donovan's Gram. p. 326.
ᵹlain, *adj. gen.*; *see under* ᵹlan.
ᵹlan, *adj., gen. m.* ᵹlain, *fem. and comp.* ᵹlaine, clean,
pure, clear, sincere, innocent.
ᵹleoir, *p. n. m.*, *Gleoir*, a man's name.
ᵹlonḋa, *p. n. m.*, *Glonda*, a man's name; aṫ-ᵹlonḋa,
Glonda's ford or river passage, *q. v. and note p.* 53.
ᵹnáċaċ, *adj., comp.* -aiᵹe, usual, constant, customary,
common; ᵹo ᵹnáċaċ, habitually.
ᵹnátach *for* ᵹnáċaċ, *q. v.*
ᵹní *for* ᵹniḃ, *q. v.*
ᵹniḃ, *v. irr., past of* ᵹniḃim *or* ḋeunaim, I do *or* make;
ᵹniḃeaḋ, *hab. past*, used to make; *also* ᵹní; ᵹní
rium, *i. e.* ḋo ᵹniḃeaḋ re.
ᵹniḃeaḋ, *hab. past*; *see under* ᵹniḃ.
ᵹnim, *obs. for* ᵹnioṁ, *q. v.*
ᵹnimarta *for* ᵹnioṁarta; *q. v. and* ᵹnioṁ.
ᵹnioṁ, *n. m.*, *gen.* -ṁa; *pl.* -ṁra *and* -ṁarta, an act, a
deed, action, exploit; mac-ᵹnioṁarta, the youthful
exploits; ᵹnioṁarta na n-apstal, the acts of the
Apostles, na ᵹ-céaḋ nᵹnioṁ, of the hundreds of
exploits.
ᵹnioṁarta, *pl. of* ᵹnioṁ, *q. v.*
ᵹní rium, *obs., see under* ᵹniḃ.
ᵹo, *prep.* (1), to, unto, till, until; (2), with, along with:
*see under* co, *and* aine; *also* ᵹion ᵹo *and* cin co:
ᵹo nᵹail, with valour.
ᵹo, *conj.* (1) that; (2) *par. before verbs*, ᵹo m-baḋ, that
may be; (3) *par. before adjectives, and occasionally
nouns form adverbs*; ᵹo maiṫ, well; *note par.* 6 *a.*
ᵹo, *adj.*, still, yet.
ᵹoḃa *for* ᵹoba, *q. v.*
ᵹoba, *n. m., gen.* -ann, *dat.* -ainn; *pl.* ᵹoiḃne, a smith;
*see* plaiṫ-ᵹoba *and* plaiṫ.

gobann *for* goba, *and* gobann; *see under* goba

gobainn, *dat. of* goba, a smith, *q. v.*

gobann, *gen. of* goba, *q. v.*

go bé rin, *see* conao **and** conro, so from that; *also, a corrupt form of* cao é rin, what is that?

goin, *v. ac., inf.* gon *and* gonab, wound; goin, *past.* (he) wounded; gonar, *hist. pres.* wounds.

goin, *past.* wounded; *see under* goin.

goiriu *v. ac.* 3*rd pers. pl., pres. ind.*, they cry, or call; *see* gáir *and par.* 56.

Goll, *p. n. m. Goll*, a man's name, the son of **Morna**.

gonar, *hist. pres.* wounds; *see* goin.

gonur *for* gonar, *q. v.*

gráo *for* gráb, love; *q. v.*

gráb, *n. m., gen. id.*, gráib *and* grába, love.

graig, *n. f. obs.*, steeds; a stud of horses.

gránoa, *adj.*, ugly, hideous; ur-gránoa, very ugly.

greannuig, *v. ac., inf.* -ugab, (1), incite, exhort; (2), challenge, defy; greannuigio, they challenge, *q. v.*

greannuigio, *v. ac.*, 3*rd. pers. pl. pres. ind., see* greannuig.

grennaigit *for* greannuigio; *q. v. and* greannuig.

guin *for* goin, *and* goin, *q. v.*

gul, *n. m., gen.* guil, *and* gola, weeping, a cry or wail.

gur, *from* go *and* ro, that (*in past tense*), *see* go.

gur, *from* go *or* gu (*r added before a vowel*), to, till; *see* go.

.1., *cont. for* eaoon, *or* 1oóon, *q. v., i.e.*, that is to say.

í, *pers. pron.*, she, her, it; *secondary form of* rí.

1, *or* a, *prep.* in; *causes eclipsis*; *see*, a, inn, ann.

1ach, *or* eo, *obs. n. m., gen. id.*, a salmon; *see* braoán, *and note, p.* 65., *par.* 51, *and also p.* 48.

1ao, *pers. pron.*, they, them; 1ao rin, those; 1ao ro, these.

1ar, (1), *adv.*, after afterwards; (2), *prep.*, at, on; 1ar rin' after that; 1ar n-a mápac, on the morrow; 1ar n-oul, after going; *causes eclipsis*; *sometimes written for* air, on, upon, *q.v.*

1arain *for* irair, *obs. q. v. and* 1arraib.

1aram, *adv., expletive*; indeed, then, moreover; *note p.* 56.

1aroain, *see* 1artain.

1aroam *for* 1artan *or* 1aram, *expl. q. v.*

1arr, *v. ac., inf.* 1arraib, ask, seek, demand; agarraib, seeking; o'1arraib, to seek; *same word as* riarruig, inquire.

1arraib, *inf. and part. of* 1arr, *q. v.*

1arraio *for* 1arraib, *q. v. and* 1arr.

1artain *or* 1artan, *adv. obs.*, afterwards, then.

ıαɲταm *for* ıαɲταın, *q. v. obs.*
ıαɲum, *obs. adv., for* ıαɲαṁ, *q. v.*
ıc *for* αʒ, *q. v.*
ıɒ *for* αɒ, ατ, ɒo, *q. v.*
ıɒıɲ, (1) *prep.* between, betwixt; *governs accusative singular and dative plural;* (2) *conj.* both; (3) *adv.* **expletive.** at all. *See note a. par* 4.
ıLe *or* ılLe, *i.e.* 1 Leıċ; *see under* Leαċ.
ım *for* ıom, um, *or* uım, *prep.* about, concerning, on.
ım *for* αm', *pr. pron., q. v.,* in my.
ım *or* αm, *form for* αn, *the article, q. v.*
ım, *an intensitive particle; see under* ımċeαċτ.
ımαch *for* αmαċ, *q. v., adv.* out; *i.e.* 'ɲα máʒ *or* α mαċ-αıɲe, in the field; *compare* αɲτeαċ, *i.e.* 'ɲα τeαċ, in the house, within; αmuıʒ, without, *and* αɲτıʒ, with-in, *which are composed of other forms of the same words, are used when a state of* rest *outside or inside is implied:* τıʒ ɲe αmαċ, he comes out.
ımáın *for* ıomáın, *q. v.*
ımαɲαıɲıum, *obs. for* αımɲıʒeαɲ, *q. v.*
ımboɲ *for* ımuɲ, *q. v. and note par.* 54.
ımbuıLe, *i.e.* ın buıLe; *see* buıLe *and* bolʒαċ.
ımɒα *for* ıombα, *q.v.*
ımɒıcɲcıɲ *from* ım, *intens.* very, *and* ɒıɲcıɲ, quick, *q. v.*
ımeαL, *n. m., gen. and pl.* -ıL, a border, edge; *see* bóɲɒ.
ımeαL-bóɲɒ, *cpd. n. m.* margin, *see* ımeαL *and* bóɲɒ.
ımɲıch, *obs. n.* a contention, a fight; *see note c, par.* 1.
ımıɲ, *v. ac., inf.* ımıɲτ, play (as at games); ımɲıɒ, 3*rd. pers. pl.* they play; ımɲıɒ, plays; ımɲım, I play.
ımıɲτ, *inf. and n. f.,* playing, play, exercise.
ımmαılLe, *i.e.,* 1 *or* α mαılLe, with, together with; *see note a. on par.* 14; m *is doubled here by a species of eclipsis.*
ımon *for* ım *or* um, *and* αn, *prep. and art.,* about the.
ımoɲɲu *for* ıomoɲɲo, *or* umoɲɲo, *q. v.*
ımɲıɒ, 3*rd. pers. sing. pres.; see under* ımıɲ.
ımɲıɒ *for* ımɲıɒ, *q. v. and* ımıɲ.
ımτeαchτ *for* ımċeαċτ, to go, *but here put for* τeαċτ, coming; *see par.* 28 *note, and* O'Don. Gram. *p.* 274.
ımuɲ, *n. obs.,* a kind of charm; *see* ımboɲ, *par.* 54 *and note*
ın, *form of* αn, the article, *sing. and pl.*
ın *or* ınn, *prep.* in; *see* 1, α, αnn, *&c.*
ınα *for* 1 n-α, in his, her, their, which, &c.
ınαɒ *for* ıonαɒ, *q. v.*
ınαɲ *for* ın αɲ, *or* αnn, *obs. int. part.,* whether?
ınɒeʒαıɒ *for* ın ɒeʒαıɒ, *i.e,.* 1 n-ɒıαıʒ; *see* ɒıαıʒ.

ınfeıneᴅᴀ *for* ınḟéınneᴀḃᴀ, *q. v.*
ınḟéınneᴀḃᴀ, *adj.* fit to rank among the Fiann.
ınġeᴀn, ⎫ *n. f., gen.* -ġıne, *pl.* -ġeᴀnᴀ, a daughter, a virgin,
ınġın,   ⎭ a woman.
ınġın *for* ınġeᴀn, *q. v.*
ınġıne, *gen. of* ınġeᴀn, *q. v.*
ınıf, *n. f., gen.* ınfe, an island; ınıf ḟáıl, one of the names of Ireland; *see* ḟáıl, *and* feᴀn.
ınn *for* ın, ᴀnn, *q. v.; also* ᴀ *and* ı, in.
ınnᴀ *for* ı n-ᴀ *or* ᴀnnᴀ; *see* ınᴀ, *and* ᴀnn.
ınnᴀᴅ *for* ıonᴀᴅ, *q. v.*
ınnıf, *v. ac., inf.* ınnfın, ınnıfın *or* ınnfe, tell, declare; ınnıfıḋ, *3rd. pers pres. tense,* tells; ınnfeᴀḋ, *past. pass.,* was told; *followed by* ᴅo, *prep.*
ınnıfıḋ, *3rd pers. pres. ind.,* ; *see under* ınnıf.
ınnfıᴅ *for* ınnfeᴀḋ, *q. v.*
ınnfeᴀḋ, *past: pass.,* was told; *see* ınnıf; ᴅo h-ınnfeᴀḋ ᴅí, it was told to her.
ınnfᴀmlᴀ *for* ıonnfámlᴀ. *q. v.*
ınnᴄı *or* ınnᴄe, *pr. pron.* in her, in it.
ınfe, *gen. of* ınıf, an island, *q. v.*
ınḟeılġe, *cpd. adj., from* ın *and* feᴀlġ, fit to lead the chase; *see par.* 18; *compare* ınḟéınneᴀḃᴀ.
ınfelġᴀ *for* ınḟeılġe, *q. v.*
ıoḋon, *adv.,* that is to say; *see* eᴀḋon *and* .ı. .
ıomáın, *v. ac., inf., id.* hurl, toss; ᴀġ ıomáın, hurling.
ıomᴀfḃᴀıḋ, *n. f., gen. id.,* a contention, a controversy; ıomᴀfḃᴀıḋ ᴄᴀᴄᴀ, a trial of battle; *(see par.* 1.), ıomᴀfḃᴀıḋ nᴀ m-báfᴅ, the contention of the bards.
ıomḋᴀ, *indec. adj.,* many, much; buḋ ıomḋᴀ, 'twas many.
ıomoffo, *conj.* also, but; *adv.* moreover, likewise; *see* umoffo; *sometimes merely expletive.*
ıonᴀᴅ, *n. m., gen. and pl.,* ıonᴀıᴅ, a place.
ıonnᴀᴅ *for* ıonᴀᴅ, a place, *q. v.*
ıonnof, *conj.,* so that, insomuch.
ıonnfámlᴀ, *gen. of* ıonnfáṁᴀıl, *q. v.*
ıonnfáṁᴀıl, (1), *n. f., gen.* -ṁlᴀ, the like, similitude; (2), *adj.,* such like, comparable; feᴀlġᴀıfe ᴀ ıonnfámlᴀ, *(gen.),* his like (or equal) as a hunter.
ıonnfuıḋe, *n. m., gen. id.,* (1), approach, meeting; (2), assault, invasion; ᴅ' ıonnfuıḋe, *cpd. prep. (governing gen. case),* towards; ᴅ'ᴀ n-ıonnfuıḋe, towards them, to meet them; ᴅ'ıonnfuıḋe Muıfne, to visit Muireann, *see* fᴀıġeᴅ.
ıonnfuıġıḋ, *3rd pers. pres, ind.,* attacks, approaches.

ıɴᴀɪꞃ *for* ɪᴀꞃꞃᴀɪᴅ, *q. v. and* ɪᴀꞃꞃ.
ɪꞃ, *assertive verb*, it is ; *secondary form of* ᴀʙ ; *past* ʙᴜᴅ *or*
    ʙᴀ ; *cond.* ʙᴀᴅ, *q. v.*, ᴅ'ᴀ ɴ-ᴀʙ, *or* ᴅᴀꞃᴀʙ, to which
    is ; ᴅ'ᴀꞃʙ, to which was ; *or* ᴅᴀꞃʙ.
ɪꞃ, *conj. for* ᴀ'ꞃ, 'ᴜꞃ *or* ᴀɢᴜꞃ, and.
ɪꞃ, *prep.* in ; *for* ᴀɴɴꞃ, *q. v. and* ᴀɴɴ.
ɪꞃᴀᴛ *for* ɪꞃ ᴛᴜ, thou art, it is thou ; *see note par.* **45.**
ɪꞃʙᴇɴᴛ *for* ᴀꞃʙᴇɴᴛ *or* ᴀᴛʙᴇɴᴛ, said.
ɪꞃɪɴ *or* ɪꞃ ɪɴ *for* ᴀɴɴꞃ ᴀɴ, *prep. and art.*, in the.
ɪꞃꞃᴇᴅ *or* ɪꞃ ꞃᴇᴀᴅ, *i.e.*, ɪꞃ ᴇᴀᴅ, it is it ; *see* ᴇᴀᴅ.
ɪᴛᴀɪᴅᴇ, *or* ɪ ᴛᴀɪᴅᴇ, in secrecy : *see* ᴛᴀɪᴅᴇ, *and* O'D. Sup.
ɪᴛᴇ *for* ɪꞃ é *or* ɪꞃ ꞃɪᴀᴅ, they are, it is they ; *see note par* 20. *and*
    O'D. Gram. *p.* 161.
ɪᴛɪꞃ *or* ɪᴛᴇꞃ *for* ɪᴅɪꞃ, *q. v.*
ʟᴀ, *i.e.*, ʟᴇ. *prep.* with, by, for ; *see* ʟᴇ *and* ꞃᴇ.
ʟᴀ́, *n. m., gen.* ʟᴀᴇ, ʟᴀᴏɪ, *dat.* ʟᴏ́ , *pl.* ʟᴀᴇᴄᴇ, ʟᴀᴇᴄᴀ, ʟᴀ́ɪᴄᴇ,
    a day, ʟᴀ́ ᴇɪʟᴇ *or* ᴀꞃᴀɪʟᴇ ʟᴀ́, another day.
**ʟᴀʙꞃᴀꞃ**, *v. ac., hist. pres. tense of* ʟᴀʙᴀɪꞃ, speaks.
**ʟᴀᴄᴀ**, *n. f., gen.* -ᴀɴ, *dat.* -ᴀɪɴ, *pl.* -ᴀɪɴ, a duck ; *see* ᴘꞃᴀꞃ-
    ʟᴀᴄᴀ ; ᴄᴏ ɴ-ᴀ ʟᴀᴄᴀɪɴ, with her (brood of) ducks.
**ʟᴀᴄᴀɪɴ**, *pl. of* ʟᴀᴄᴀ, *q. v.*
**ʟᴀᴇᴄʜ** *for* ʟᴀᴏᴄ, *q. v.*
ʟᴀᴇᴄꞃɪᴅ *for* ʟᴀᴏᴄꞃᴀɪᴅ, heroes, *q. v.*
ʟᴀ́ɢᴀɪɢ, *p. n. m., Laghaigh*, a man's name.
ʟᴀɪᴄʜ *for* ʟᴀᴏɪᴄ, *gen. and pl., q. v.*
ʟᴀɪᴅɪꞃ, *adj. comp.*, ʟᴀɪᴅꞃᴇ, strong.
ʟᴀɪᴅ *for* ʟᴀɪɢ *or* ʟᴀᴏɪᴅ, *q. v.*
ʟᴀɪɢ *for* ʟᴀᴏɪᴅ, a poem, *q. v.*
ʟᴀɪɢᴀɪɢ *for* ʟᴀ́ɢᴀɪɢ, *q. v.*
ʟᴀɪɢᴇᴀɴ, *n. m., Laighean*, Leinster ; *see note par.* 48.
ʟᴀɪɢᴇɴ *for* ʟᴀɪɢᴇᴀɴ, Leinster, *q. v.*
ʟᴀ́ɪᴍ, *dat. of* ʟᴀ́ᴍ, a hand ; *q. v.*
ʟᴀɪᴍ *for* ʟᴀ́ɪᴍ ; *see* ʟᴀ́ᴍ.
**ʟᴀ́ɪᴍᴅᴇᴀꞃɢ**, *cpd. adj.*, red-handed.
ʟᴀ́ɪɴ, *old acc. form for* ʟᴀ́ɴ, *adj. q. v.*
ʟᴀɪꞃ *for* ʟᴇɪꞃ, *q. v.*, *also* ʟᴏ *and* ʟᴀ.
ʟᴀɪꞃɪᴅᴇ *for* ʟᴇɪꞃ-ꞃᴇᴀɴ ; *see* ʟᴇɪꞃ *and* ʟᴇ.
**ʟᴀ́ᴍ**, *v. ac., inf.* -ᴀᴅ, (1), dare, presume ; (2), handle, man-
    age, take in hand ; ɴɪᴏꞃ ʟᴀ́ᴍ, did not dare.
ʟᴀᴍ *for* ʟᴀ́ᴍ, *v. and for* ʟᴀ́ᴍ, *n.*, *q. v.*
**ʟᴀ́ᴍ**. *n. f., gen.* ʟᴀ́ɪᴍᴇ, *dat.* ʟᴀ́ɪᴍ, a hand ; ʟᴇ ʟᴀ́ɪᴍ**ɪɢᴀᴄ** ꞃɪɢ,
    by the hand of every king.
ʟᴀᴍᴅᴇᴀꞃɢ *for* ʟᴀ́ɪᴍᴅᴇᴀꞃɢ, *q. v.*
ʟᴀᴍꞃᴀɪɢᴇ, *p. n. m. Lamhraighe*, name of a district.
ʟᴀᴍꞃᴀɪɢᴇ *for* ʟᴀᴍꞃᴀɪɢᴇ, *q. v.*

Lán, *adj., comp.* Láine, full, complete.
Laoċ, *n. m., gen. and pl.* Laoiċ, a warrior, a hero.
Laoċṗaiḋ, *n. m. pl.* a band or company of heroes or champions; Laoċṗaiḋ Luaiġne, the warriors of Luaighne; *see note d. par.* 1.
Laoġa, *p. n. m., see* ṫeinm-Laoġa, *and note par.* 54.
Laoiḋ, *n. f., gen.* Laoiḋe, *pl.* Laoiḋṫe, *and* Laoiḋeanna, a lay, a poem; compare *lay*, English, and *lied*, German.
Laṫ *for* Leaṫ, *q. v.*
Le, *prep.* with, by, to, for; *see* La, ṗe, *note par.* 14 *a. and* 44.
Le, *i.e.*, iLe *or* iLLe, *q. v. for* Leiṫ, *see under* Leaṫ.
Léan, *pr. n. m.* Léan déad-ġheal, *or*, of the white-teeth, a celebrated Danann artificer, who gave name to Loċ Léim, *q. v.*
Lean, *v. ac., inf.* -naṁain, follow, continue, Lean ḋe, follow on, persevere; ḋo Lean an ṫ-ainm ḋe, the name stuck to him.
Leanaḋ *for* Lean, *q. v.* followed.
Leaṫaiḋ, *obs. for* Leaṫnuiġiḋ, *q. v.*
Leaṫ, *pr. pron.*, with thee.
Leaṫ, *n. f., gen.* Leiṫe, *pl.* Leaṫanna, a half, a side, a moiety; one of a pair; Leaṫ-ṗorg, *or* Leaṫ-ṗúil, one eye; Leaṫ ṗúile, half an eye; Leaṫ cluiċe, half of a game; a Leaṫ-ṫaoiḃ, on one side; ṗá Leiṫ, severally; aiṗ Leiṫ, apart; a Leiṫ, *id.*, ó ṗin a Leiṫ, from that time to this; (*see* iLLe); ḋo Leiṫ, in regard of; Leaṫ-ṗiaṗ, westward, &c. (*Idioms.*)
Leaṫ-cluiċe, *cpd. n. f., see under* Leaṫ.
Leaṫnuiġiḋ, 3rd pers. pres. ind. of Leaṫnuiġ, spreads out.
Leaṫ-ṗúil, *cpd. n. f.,* one eye; *see under* Leaṫ.
Léi *pr. pron.* with her, by her.
Léim, *gen. of* Léan; *see* Loċ Léim *and* Léan.
Leiṗ, *pr. pron.* with him, by him; Leiṗ-ṗean, *emph.*; Leiṗ ṗin, with that; *see* Le *and* ṗe.
Leiṫ, *dat. of* Leaṫ, half, *q. v.*
Leo, *pr. pron.* with them; Leo-ṗan, *emph.*
Leṫ *for* Leaṫ *and* Leiṫ; *see under* Leaṫ.
Leṫ-cluiċe *for* Leaṫ-cluiċe, *see under* Leaṫ.
Leṫ-ṗorc *for* Leaṫ-ṗorg, *or* Leaṫ-ṗúil; *see under* Leaṫ.
Liaṫ, *p. n. m., Liath*, a man's name; gray; Liath Luachra, the *liath* of Luachair; Liath Màcha, the *liath* or *gray-one* of Macha.
Liṗe, *p. n. f. gen. id.,* life, the river Liffey.
Lil, *v. obs.,* followed; *see* Lean.
Linġiḋ *for* Linġiḋ, *q. v.*

Lingiḋ, 3rd pers. pres. ind. of Ling, leaps, plunges, flings, Lingiḋ-ṗin for Lingiḋ ṗéiṗeaṅ, emph. he bounds.
Lingioṗin, obs. form, see under Lingiḋ.
Linn, pr. pron., with us; Linne, emph.
Linne, emp. pr. pron., with ourselves; see under Linn.
Liom, pr. pron., with me; see Le; Liom-ṙa, emph.
Liom-ṙa, emph. pr. pron. with myself; see Liom.
Ló, dat. of Lá. a day; q. v.
Loċ, n. m., gen. and pl., Loċa, a lake, a *loch*; Loċ Léin, the Lakes of Killarney, chiefly the upper lake, see Léin and Léaṅ.
Loċ-Léin, n. m., see Loċ, Léaṅ, and Léin.
Loċán, p. n. m., gen. -áin, *Lochan*, par. 37.
Loin, pl. of Lon, q. v.
Loiṙceṙ for Loiṙgeaṙ, q. v.
Loiṙgeaṙ, 1st. pers. sing. past of Loiṙg, I burned,
Lon, n. m., gen. and pl., Loin or Luin, a blackbird.
Lonḋ or Lonn, adj. obs., bold, powerful.
Long, Luṅg, } n. m. pl. Longa, a stave, a staff, a club, a log of wood, ḋo ċuiṙeaḋaṙ a Longa ḋ'uṙċuṙ aiṙ, they aimed their sticks in a cast at him; compare Luṅg-feaṙṙaiḋ, a spindle-pole, in "*Tír na n-óg.*"
Longa, pl. of Long, q. v.
Luaċaiṙ p. n. f., gen. Luaċṙa, *Luachair*; note b. par. 33.
Luaċṙa, p. n. gen. of Luaċaiṙ, q. v.; rushy, Ceaṁaiṙ Luaċṙa, see note 2 b. and 11 b.; taṙ Sliaḃ Luaċṙa, over *Sliabh Luachra*; see note b. par. 33.
Luaicṅe for Luaċṙa, q. v. and Luaċaiṙ.
Luaiġne, p. n. pl., dat. -niḃ, the *Luaighne*; see note d. par. 1.
Luaiġni, *Luaighni*; see Luaiġne.
Luaiġniḃ, dat. pl. of Luaiġne, q. v.
Luaṫ, adj. comp. Luaiṫe, pl. Luaṫa, swift, quick.
Luaṫ for Luaṫ, q. v.
Luḋ, v. obs., play, exercise.
Luiġech for Luiḋeaċ; see Luġaiḋ.
Luġaiḋ, p. n. m., gen. Luiġeaċ and Luiġioċ *Lughaidh*, a man's name
Luiċet, p. n. m., *Luichet*, a man's name.
Luiċet for Luiċet, q. v.
Luiḋ, obs., for Luiḋ, went, q. v.
Luiḋ, obs. v., go; Luiḋ-ṙium for ḋo ċuaiḋ ṙe or ḋo Luiḋ, he went; see O'D. Gram., p. 259.
Luiḋ ṙium, obs. v. emph.; see under Luiḋ.
Luiġeaċ or Luiġioċ, gen. of Luġaiḋ, q. v.
Luin for Loin, pl. of Lon, q. v.

lúťṁap, *adj., comp.* -aiṗe, nimble, active.
m', *contr. for* mo, my, *before a vowel.*
má, *conj.* if, (*see* maṫ *and* má'ṗ).
mac, *n. m., gen. and voc.* mic *or* meic, *pl.* maca, *dat. pl.*
  macaiḃ, (1) a son ; (2) a boy ; (3) a descendant ; (4)
  *used adjectively,* boyish, youthful ; mac-ġníoṁapċa,
  youthful actions ; (5) a copy ; mac leaḃaiṗ, copy
  of a book. (*Idioms.*)
macaiḃ *for* macaiḃ, *q. v. and* mac.
macaiḃ, *dat. pl. of* mac, *q. v.*
macaem *for* macaoṁ, *q. v.*
**macaoṁ**, *n. m. gen.* -aoiṁ, *pl. id. and* -aoṁa, a child, a
  youth, a lad, a young man ; macaoṁ-mná, a young
  woman.
macġnimapċa *for* mac-ġníoṁapċa, *q. v.*
mac-ġníoṁapċa, *cpd. n.* youthful exploits ; boyish feats :
  *see* mac *and* ġníoṁ.
macpaiṫ *for* macpaiṫ, *q. v.*
macpaiṫ, *coll. n. m.* youths : an macpaiṫ óġ, the youth.
maṫ *obs. for* má *or* máṗ, *q. v.*
maṫ *for* máġ, *q. v.*
maṫ-peṫa *for* máġ-peaṫa, *q. v.*
mael *for* maol, *q. v.*
maenmuiġ *for* maonṁáġ, *q. v.*
maepaiġeċt, *for* maopaċt, *q. v.*
**máġ**, *n. m., gen.* máiġe, muiġe, *and* máġa ; *pl.* máġa, a
  field, a plain ; *Welsh* maes. máġ-peaṫa, plain of the
  wood ; máġ-life, plain of the Liffey ; names of
  places ; sometimes feminine.
maġ *for* máġ, *q. v.*
máġ-peaṫa, *see under* máġ *and* peaṫa.
máġ-life, *p. n. m. Magh-life, see* máġ.
maiġe, *gen. of* máġ, *q. v. and compare* teaċ, *m., gen.* tiġe.
maille, *prep.* with, along with ; maille le *or* pe ; *see note
  a. par.* 14 ; together with ; a maille *id.*
maol, *adj. comp.* maoile, (1) bald, tonsured ; (2) horn-
  less, pointless ; (3) blunt, bare ; (4) humble ;
  *n. m.* a servant, a devotee, a person dedicated,
  as maol-muiṗe, *&c. ;* Ueimne maol, Deimne
  the bald.
maonṁáġ, *p. n. m. Maonmhagh ; see par.* 46 *and note.*
maopaċt, *n. f.* stewardship, wardenship.
mápaċ, *n. m. gen. id. and* -aiġ, the morrow ; *see* bápaċ
  *and par.* 25, *and note ; also* iap ; a mápaċ,
  to-morrow.

mar (1), *conj.* as, even as; (2), *prep.* as, for, like; (3), *adv.* mar a, where; in Scotch Gaelic *far a*, mar an g-ceuóna, as the same; mar a céile, as its fellow, *i.e.* likewise; mar rın, as that; mar ro, as this, *i.e.* so, thus; mar aon, as one, together; mar aon leo together with them. (*Idioms*.)

marb, *v. ac., inf.*; -baó, kill, slay; no marb, *past*, killed; oo marb re, he slew; marbaıó-re, *imp. emph. pl.*, kill (ye); marbaó, *past.* was slain; muırrıóe, cond, *pass.*, may be slain; (ut marbtar, *obs.*).

marb *for* marb, *adj. or v. q. v.*

marb, *adj.*, dead, slain.

marb, *past tense of* marb, *q. v.*

marbaıó-rıoe *for* marbaıó-re, *q. v., and* marb.

marbaıó-re, *imp. emph.*, of marb, *q. v.*

marbaó *for* marbaó, *q. v.*

marbaó, (oo), *inf. ac. of* marb, *q. v.,* to slay (*act. for pass.*) *see note on p.* 45: m'aon mac oo marbaó, that my only son was slain.

marbta *for* marbta, *q. v., and* marbaó.

marbta, *gen. of n. m.* marbaó, *q. v.*

marbaó, *v. n. m., gen.* marbta, killing, slaying, murder; aır tí oo marbta, watching to slay thee.

marbtar, *obs.* for marbtar *or* muırrıóe; *see* marb.

má'r (*for* má *and* ır *q. v.*), if it is.

mátaır, *n. f., gen.* mátar, *pl.* máıtre, a mother.

matáır *for* mátaır, a mother, *q. v.*

meaóon *for* meaóon, *q. v.*

meaóon, *n. m., gen.*, -oın, the midst, the middle; meaóon- múma (*adjectively*), mid-Munster; *or* meaóon múman, middle of Munster, meaóon-laoı, mid-day, meaóon-oıóce, mid-night.

meoóon *for* meaóon, the middle, *q. v.*

menech, *obs.* for m'éınea¿, *see under* éınea¿.

mıc, *gen.* and *voc. sing.* and *nom. pl.* (also maca), son, sons; a mıc *or* a meıc (*voc.*) O Son, *see under* mac.

mıll *for* mıll, destroyed, *q. v.*

mıll, *v. past* tense, destroyed; gur mıll re, that he destroyed.

mná, *gen.* and *pl.* of bean, a woman, *q. v.*

mnaı, *obs. acc. form of* bean, a woman.

mnaoı, *dat. sing. of* bean, a woman; (*irregular noun*).

mo, *poss. pron.*, my; *contracted* m' *before a vowel*.

mó, *comp.* and *superl.* of mór, great; *q. v.*

móirḟeireaṅ, n. m., seven, seven persons; *from* mór, great; and reireaṅ, six persons; *i.e.* the big six.
mo nuaṙ, *interj.*, alas! woe! *see* nuaṙ.
mór, *adj., gen. m.* móir, *f.* móire; *comp.* mó *and* mórḋe, great, big, large; níor mó, more; ir mó, most.
Mórna, *p. n. m.*, *Morna*, a man's name; father of Goll, and ancestor of *Clanna* Morna; mic Mórna, sons of Morna.
morrerir *for* móirḟeireaṅ, seven, *q. v.*
muc, *n. f., gen.* muice, *pl.* muca, a pig, swine.
mucc *for* muc, *q. v*,
muicc, *old form for dative of* maġ, *q. v.*
muicce *for* muice, *q. v.*
muice, *gen*, *of* muc, a pig, *q. v.*
muiġe, *gen. of* maġ. *q. v. and* maiġe.
Muireaḋaċ, *gen.* -aiġ, *p. n. m.*, *Muireadhach*, a man's name.
Muireaḋaiġ *for* Muireaḋaiġ, *q. v.*
Muireaḋaiġ, *gen. of* Muireaḋaċ, *q. v.*
Muireann, *p. n. f., gen. and old acc.* Muirne, **Muireann,** a woman's name.
ṁuirrḋe, *cond. pass. of* marḃ, kill, *q. v., and note par.* 36.
mnirn *for* múirneaċt, caressing, *q. v.*
múirnín, *n. m.*, a darling; *from* muirn.
múirneaċt, *n. f.* caressing, fondling; múirnineaċt, *id.*
Muirne, *gen. and old acc. form of* muireann, *q. v.*
Múṁa, *p. n. f., gen.* -ṁan, *dat.* -ṁain. Munster; meaḋon-ṁúṁa, middle Munster; Muiṁneaċ, a Munsterman.
mún-ċaoṁ, *adj. m. and f.* fair-necked, *as* Mórna mún-ċaoṁ, Muireann mún-ċaoṁ; *par.* 2 *and* 3, *and note*.
munċaim *for* mún-ċaoṁ, *q. v.*
Mumun *old form for* Múṁa, *q. v.*
n-a *for* a, who, which, his, her, &c.; *euphonic*.
na, *gen. f. and pl. of* an, the article, *q. v.*
na *for* ná, *imp. sign. q. v.*
na *for* 'na, *i.e.*, a n-a; *see* 'na.
ná, *neg. part., before Imperative Mood;* do not, let **not**.
'ná, *conj., form of* ioná, than.
na *for* anna, a n-a, *or* ionn a, in his, her, its, their.
naċ, *neg. rel. pron.*, who not, which not, that not; *int.* whether not; naċar, *or* ná'r, *from* ná *or* naċ *and* ro, in past time, that may not, let not.
naċar, *see under* naċ, ná'r, *and* ná.
n-aġ, *euphonic for* aġ, *q. v., and par.* 31:
n-aill, *euphonic for* aill, *q. v. and* eile.

naimoige *for* námavać, hostile, *q. v. and par.* 14.
námavać, *adj., comp.* -vaige, hostile, violent.
naonbap, *n. m.*, nine, nine individuals.
napuc *for* ná'p *or* naćap, *and* ac, vo, *or* po, *q. v.* ; that may not ; [napuc mapbcap] naċ muippíve, that may not be slain ; *cond. see note, par.* 36.
ná'p, *contracted for* naċap, *q. v.*
neaċ, *ind. pron.*, one, anyone, someone.
neich *for* neaċ, *q. v.*
neimnech *for* nimneaċ, *adj. q. v.*
neincigiup *or* neincigeap ; *i.e.*, eioipveaLuigeap *(rel. form)* [which] distinguish ; compare O'Donovan's Supp., nemċep, distinction, &c. ; and O'Reilly, nimċa, not alike, &c.
nell *for* neull, *q. v.*
neull, } *n. m., gen.* néil, a trance, a fit, a swoon;
neul, } caim-neull, the death agony.
ngniom, *gen. pl. of* gniom, *q. v. and* ngnim, *par.* 11.
ní, *neg. adv.*, not ; ni bpeug (*for* noċa), it is no lie.
ní ip *for* mò ip, *see* níop ; *sign of comparative.*
nív, } *n. m., gen. id., and* neiċe, *pl.* neiċe, *gen. pl.*
ní  } neiċeav, a thing, a matter, an affair ; gaċ nív, everything.
nimneaċ, *adj., comp.* -nige, *from* nim, poison ; (1), venomous, poisonous ; (2), fierce, passionate, peevish, disagreeable ; *see par.* 14.
niop, *neg. par. before past tense, from* ní *and* po, not.
nip *for* niop, *neg. par.* not, *q. v.*
nico, *obs. neg. par.* no, not ; *see* noċa *and* O'D. Gram., *p.* 324 ; *see par.* 53.
no, *conj.* or, nor ; no go *pres.* no gup, *past*, until.
nocha, *neg.* not, no, *see* ni, *and par.* 7 ; *also* O'Don. Giam. *p.* 324 ; *see par.* 54.
noċan, *see* noċa *and* ni, *neg. adv.* not.
nom, *obs. par. for* an, whether ? *(causing eclipsis)*, nom gavoaip, *for* an ngavoaoip, would they take ; *see par.* 18, *and* O'D. Supp. *in voce.*
nomgavoaip, *old form* ; *see* nom *and* gab.
nonbup *for* naonbap, nine, *q. v.*
nuap, *obs. n. m.* woe, sorrow ; *now used as an interjection*, mo nuap, *or* mo nuaip ! *(voc.)*. alas !
ó, *prep.* from ; ó'n, *for* ó an, from the ; ó pom a Leiċ, from that (time) out ; thenceforward.
ó, *adv.* since ; ó ċápla, since it has happened ; whereas.
ú *or* ua, *q. v., n. m., gen. and pl.* uí, a descendant.

obann, *adj. comp.* oibne, sudden ; 50 h-obann, suddenly.
oc *for* ag, *prep.* at, *q. v.*
Oche *for* Oiċe, *q. v.* (*Corca*) *Oiche.*
ocum *for* agam, *pr. pron.* at me; *q. v.*
ocur, *or* acur, *conj.* ; *old forms of* agur, and, *q. v.*
óg, *adj., comp.* óige, young ; an macpaiḃ óg, the youth.
Oiċe, *p. n. m. Oiche, i.e.* Corca-Oiche ; *see par.* **1,** *and* Conċa.
oil, *v. a., inf.* oileaṁain, bring up, educate, nourish ; ɖo h-oileaḃ, *past pass.* was reared ; ɖ'oil, *ac.* **3rd.** *pers. past.* reared.
oileaḃ, *pass. past. of* oil, *v. ac., q. v.*
Oilpe, *p. n. m.*, *Oilpe*, a man's name, *see par.* 20.
óip, *conj.* for, because ; óip buḃ ḃioḃ-ran, for it was from those, (*par.* 1); óip ir leat-ra an piogaċt, for thine is the kingdom, &c.
oip, aip, *and* ap *for* óip ; *see* óip *and* aip.
ol, *obs. def. v.*, *for* ap, says ; *see under* ap.
on *for* an, *art.*, the ; *see* imon *and* an.
on, *expletive,* indeed ; *see par.* **14** *and note a. on par.* **4.**
ón *for* ó'n, from the ; *q. v.*
ó'n, *prep. and art.*, ó *and* an, from the.
op *and* ol, **obs.** *def. v. for* ap, says ; *see under* ap.
opɖain, *obs. form of* ópɖóg, a thumb, *q. v.*
ópɖóg, *n. f., gen.* -óige, *pl.* -óga, a thumb, also a great toe ; ɖo loirgear m'ópɖóg, *par.* 53.
ópɖu, *old form of* ópɖóg, a thumb, *q. v.*
ópɖuigeaḃ, *v. ac., pass. past tense,* was ordered, entrusted, appointed ; *see* epḃaɖ *and par.* **52.**
oppa, *per. pron.*, **on** them.
opt, *pr. pron*, **on** thee opt-ra, *emphatic.*
optra, *emph. pr. pron., see under* opt.
orna, *obs. n. see under* imur, *and note on par.* 54.
ór *or* uar, *prep.* over, above ; ór luaċair, over Luachair.
pór, *v. ac., inf.* pórad, marry ; pórai, 3*rd.* **pers. pres. tense,** marries; pór, *past,* married ; *see par.* **13** *and* **38,** *and note par.* 38.
pór, *past tense of* pór, married ; *see* pór.
pórai, 3*rd pers. pres. tense of* pór, *q. v.*
ppar, *see* pparlaċa, *and notes on par.* 19.
pparlaċa, *n. f., gen.* -an, *pl.* -ain, a duck, a wild fowl, a widgeon ; *see* ppar *and* laċa ; *also notes on par.* 19.
pparlaċa *for* pparlaċa, *q. v.*
pa, *par. for* po, *pase tense, q. v.*
paɖ, *obs.* give, bring, put ; *see* Gram.: Fourke, *p.* 52 ; **O'D.** 259.

ṗáḋ, *n. m., gen. id. and* ṗáıḋ; *pl.* ṗáıṫċe, a saying
ṗaṿ, *old form for* ṗáḋ, *n. m*, a saying, *q. v.*
ṗaṿuṗ, *obs. v. past tense*, I put ; *see* ṗaṿ.
ṗaıḃ, *past tense (sec. form) of* ṿo ḃeıṫ ; was ; ní ṗaıḃ, was not, &c. ; *sometimes written* ṗaḃ.
ṗáınıc, *v. irreg. past tense (of* ṗıġım); he reached.
ṗáınıcc *for* ṗáınıc, *q. v.*
ṗaınn, *n. m., pl. of* ṗann, verses ; *also* ṗanna.
ṗála, *i.e.,* ṗo la, *obs. v., past tense*, put, sent ; *see* O'Don. Gram. *p.* 259, *and note on v.* 10. " *Tír na n-og,*" *p.* 93. *Also* took place, was arranged, happened, chanced.
ṗanna, *n. m., for* ṗaınn, *pl. of* ṗann, a verse ; *see* ṗaınn.
ṗaċ, *obs. v. past*, brought, gave; *see* ṗaṿ.
ṗaṫaım *or* ṗaṿaım, *obs. v.* I give up, deliver; *(see* O'R.), I give, I bring ; O'Don. Supp. to Dict. ; *see* ṗaṿ.
ṗe, *prep.*, with, by, for; *see* le, ṗrı, &c.; ġaċ ṗe ṗeaċṫ alternately ; *see note on par.* 44. *p,* 63 ; ṗe lınn, in (the) time of ; ṗe ṿo lınn, during thy time ; ṗe ṗılıḋeaċṫ, for (learning) poetry.
ṗé, ṗae, } *n. f., gen. id., pl.* ṗée, ṗéċe (1), time, a space of time, (2), duration, (3) the moon : le ṗé ṗaṿa, during a long time.
ṗe *for* ṗor, *or* ṗo, *see* ṗo.
ṗean, *n. m., pl.* ṗeana, a star, a planet.
ṗeana, *pl. of* ṗean, (*for* ṗeulṫ) ; *see* ṗean.
ṗée *for* ṗé *or* ṗae, *q. v.*; *and* caoın-ṗé.
Reġna, *p. n. m. Regna,* a man's name.
ṗeıḋ, *adj.* (1) smooth, level ; (2) ready, finished with ; (3) agreed, reconciled : ṗeıḋ-ṗıan, a smooth course.
ṗeıṿ *for* ṗeıḋ, *q. v.*
ṗeıḋ-ṗıan, *cpd. n. m.,* smooth course ; *see* ṗeıḋ.
ṗeıṁe *for* ṗoıṁe, *q. v.*
ṗeṗ *for* ṗıṗ *and* leıṗ, *q. v.*
ṗı *or* ṗıġ, *n. m., pl.* ṗıġċe, a king.
ṗıaċṫ, *past tense of irr. v.* ṗıġım, I reach : ġo ṗıaċṫ ṗo, till he reached; *i.e.,* ṗáınıc *or* ṗaınıġ, *q. v. and* O'D. Gram. *p.* 245.
ṗıan, *n. m.,* a course, a way, a path.
ṗıġ *or* ṗıoġ, *n. m., gen. id., pl.* ṗıġċe, a king.
ṗıġne, *v. irr. (past indic. of* ṿeun), did, made.
ṗınne, *see* ṗıġne, ṿeun, *and* ġnıḋ, did, made.
ṗınneaṿaṗ, *3rd. pers. pl. past indic of irr. v.* ṿeun, they made, did ; ıaṗ ṗın ṿo ṗınneaṿaṗ ṗíoṫ, then they made peace.
ṗıṗ, *pr. pron.* with him, by him ; *see* leıṗ.

8

ꞃꞇ, *v. ac. inf. and part id.* run ; ᴀᴦ ꞃꞇ, rur**nin** ⁊.
ꞃꞇʜ *for* ꞃꞇ, running, *q. v.*
ꞃꞇʜᴀɪᴅ *for* ꞃꞇɪᴅ, *and* ꞃꞇɪᴅ, *q. v*.,
ꞃꞇʜɪᴅ *for* ꞃꞇɪᴅ *and* ꞃꞇɪᴅ, *q. v.*
ꞃꞇɪᴅ, *3rd pers. pres. tense, ind. of* ꞃꞇ, *v. ac.* runs, *q.* ⁊. ;
    ꞃꞇɪᴅ ꞃᴇ ᴏꞃꞃᴀ, he runs on them.
ꞃꞇɪᴅ, *3rd pl. pres. ind. of* ꞃꞇ, they run.
ꞃó, *intensitive par.* very, exceeding, too; ꞃó-ꞇꞃᴇᴜꞃ, very
    brave; ꞃó-ꞃáꞃ, very excellent, exceeding fine; *ad-
    jectives do not admit of being compared when an inten-
    sitive particle is prefixed.*
ꞃo, *par. before verbs, past tense; same as* ᴅo, *q. v.*
ꞃó-ʙáɪᵹ [ꞃo-ʙᴀɪᵹ]; *see under* ʙáɪᵹ *and* ʙáᵹ.
ꞃo-ᴄᴀᴇᴍ *for* ꞃó-ᴄᴀoᴍ, *q. v.*
ꞃó-ᴄᴀoᴍ, *adj.* exceeding beautiful, very fair; *see* ᴄᴀoᴍ.
ꞃoᴄᴀɪꞃ, *obs. v.* (1), fall; (2), kill, slay ; ᴅo ꞃoᴄᴀɪꞃ ʟᴇ ᴍᴀᴄ
    Móꞃꞃᴀ, was slain by Morna's son; ꞃoᴄᴀɪꞃ, *n.* deat ,
    a fall, (O'Reilly) : ᴀꞇ ꞃoᴄʜᴀɪꞃ ᴀꞃꞃ (O'Don. Supp.
    *in voce* ʟᴇᴀꞃᴛᴀꞃ), poured or spilled out ; *see par.* 7,
    *and* 11 *and notes.*
ꞃoᴄʜᴀɪꞃ, *for* ꞃoᴄᴀɪꞃ, *q. v.*
Roᵹéɪꞃ, *p. n. m. Roigein*, a man's name.
ꞃoɪᴍᴇ, *prep.* (1), before ; (2) *pr. pron.*, before him ; ꞃoɪᴍᴇ
    ꞃɪꞃ, before that ; ʟᴜɪᴅ, *or* ᴄᴜᴀɪᴅ ꞃᴇ ꞃoɪᴍᴇ, he went
    on ; ᴄᴜɪꞃ ꞃoɪᴍᴇ, determine. (*Idioms.*) Roɪᴍᴇ *refers
    both to time and position.*
ꞃoɪꞃꞃ *for* ꞃɪꞃꞃ, ꞃɪꞃꞃᴇ, *or* ꞃɪᵹꞃᴇ, *see* ꞃɪᵹꞃᴇ.
ꞃoɪꞃꞃᴇ *for* ꞃɪꞃꞃᴇ, *or* ꞃɪᵹꞃᴇ, *q. v.*
ꞃoꞃꞃꞃᴀᴛᴀꞃ, *obs. for* ꞃɪꞃꞃᴇᴀᴅᴀꞃ, they made, *q. v.*
ꞃoꞃ *for* ꞃo *see* ꞃo *and* ᴅo.
ꞃo ꞃᴀɪꞃ *for* ꞃó-ꞃáꞃ, *q. v.*, *and* ꞃó ; *also* ꞃáꞃ.
ꞃó-ꞃáꞃ, *adj. intensitive*, exceeding fine ; *see* ꞃó *and* ꞃáꞃ ;
    *double superlative.*
ꞃoꞃᴄ *for* ꞃoꞃᵹ, *q. v.*
ꞃoꞃᵹ, *n. m.*, *gen.* ꞃoɪꞃᵹ, the eye, eyesight ; *used in poetry;
    see* ꞃúɪʟ, *and note a on par.* 4.
ꞃoꞃ ꞃᴜᴄ, *obs. v. see* ꞃoꞃᴛᴜᵹ, ꞃo ᴄᴜᵹ *and* ᴄᴜᵹ.
ꞃoꞃ ᴄᴜᵹ *for* ꞃo ᴄᴜᵹ *or* ᴄᴜᵹ, *past tense of* ʙᴇɪꞃɪᴍ *irr gular
    verb, gave ; see also* ꞃᴜᵹ, bore.
ꞃó-ᴛꞃᴇᴜꞃ, *cpd. adj.*, very brave ; *see* ꞃó.
ꞃᴜᵹ, *v. irr.*, *past tense of* ʙᴇɪꞃɪᴍ, bore, brought forth.
ꞃᴜɪᴅɪᵹ, *n. obs.* brilliance, brilliancy, O'D. : *compare* O'R.
    ꞃᴜɪᴅᴇᴀᴅ, a ray of light.
ꞃᴜꞃ *for* ꞃo ; *see* ꞃo *and* ᴅo.
Rᴜꞇ, *p. n. m.*, *Ruth*, a man's name.

ra, *emphatic suffix* ; liom-ra, with me ; *see* re.
raigeo *for* ruide *in* ionnruide, *n. m. and cpd.*, *prep. q. v.*
raigio *for* raigeo *or* ruide ; *see* ionnruide.
ráile, *n. m. and f., gen. id.*, the sea.
ráime *for* ráiṁe, *n. f., q. v. and* ráṁ.
ráiṁe, *n. f., gen. id.* pleasure, ease, quiet.
rain *for* rán, *q. v. and* ró-rán.
ral *for* ráile, *q. v.*
raltair, *n. f., gen.* -trac, *pl.* -traca, (1) *a* Saltair *or* chronicle, *often metrical* ; (2) the Psalms ; *see notes pp.* 46 *and* 54.
raltrac, *n. f., gen. of* raltair, *q. v.*
ram *for* ráṁ, *n. or* ráṁ, *adj. q. v.*
ráṁ, *adj.* ; *comp. and abstract noun* ráiṁe, pleasant, happy, easy ; ruanán ráṁ *or* ruanán ráiṁe, pleasant slumber, *or* slumber of pleasure.
**ráṁ,** *n. m.*, summer, summer-time, the sun : rán-ráṁ, **noble** summer : ráṁ-ruaill, summer swallows.
ráṁail, *n. f., gen.* -ṁla, manner, likeness, the like.
ráṁail, *adj. comp.* -ṁla, like, such.
Samain, *n. f., gen.* Saṁna, *Samhain* **(November)** ; *see note par.* 56 *a. p.* 69.
ráṁla *adj.* like ; *see* ráṁail *and* ionnráṁla.
ramlaid *for* ráṁail, *n. f. q. v.*
ráṁ-ruaill, *n. m. pl.*, **summer** swallows ; *see* ráṁ.
ran, *emph. suffix*, a cuat-ran, his tribe or race.
rán, *intensitive par.* very, excellent, great, &c. ; *see* ró *and* ró-rán : *also* ráṁ, rán-ṫean, an excellent man ; rán-luiṫṁan, very nimble.
rán-ráṁ, *cpd. n. m.*, noble summer ; *see* ráṁ.
rceill *or* rcill, *obs. adj.* quick, sudden ; *see under* oirgell.
rcéit, *v. n. m., gen. id.* vomiting, putting forth ; rcéit rola, a shower of blood.
rcéla, *n. m. pl. for* rceula, *q. v.*
rceula, *n. m. pl. and* rceulta, **stories,** tidings, **news.**
re, *pers. pron.* he, it ; reirean, *emph.*
ré, *num. adj. card.* six.
re *or* ri, *emphatic suffix after a final slender vowel*.
reacṫ, *num. adj. card.* seven (*causes eclipsis.*).
reacṫṁain, *n. f., gen.* -ṁaine, *pl. id.* a week ; a g-ceann reacṫṁaine, at the **end** of a week.
realg, *n. f., gen.* roilge, *dat.* reilg, *pl.* realga, a chase, a hunt ; ir riad rin do ġniṫead realga dó, it is they used to hunt for him : *par.* 48 ; an ceud ṫealg the first chase ; in-ṫeilge fully trained for the chase.

realga, *pl. of* realg, *q. v.*
realgaire, *n. m., gen. id., pl.* -ribe, a hunter.
rean, *adj.* old; (*comes before the noun*).
rean, *written for* ran, *q. v., after a final slender vowel.*
reanchaib *for* reancaibe, *q. v.*
reancaibe, *n. m., gen. id.*, an historian, an antiquary.
reanouine, *n. m.*, an old man; *see* ouine, *and note on par.*
  31; an vá feanouine; the two old persons.
rean-féinn, *dat. of* rean-fiann, *q. v.*
rean-fiann, *n. f., gen.* -féinne; old Fianns; *see* fiann.
reanóir, *n. m., gen.* -óra, an old man, an elder.
rect *for* react, seven, *q. v.*
rechtmuine *for* reactmaine; *see* reactmain.
réo, *n. m. obs.* a road, a path; *see note on par.* 44.
reilge, *n. f., gen. of* realg, *q. v.*
rein *for* rean, old, *q. v.* (*before a slender vowel.*)
rein-féinn *for* rean-féinn, *q. v. and* rean-fiann.
rein-fiann, *also written* rean-fiann, *q. v.*
reircinn *or* reirgeann, *n. m. or f.*, a marsh, a fen, a boggy
  place; a reirginn fuair, in a cold marsh.
réiream *for* reirean, *q. v.*
reirean, *emph. pers. pron.* he; *see* re.
relg *for* realg, *q. v.*
relga *for* realga, *q. v. and* realg.
relgaire *for* realgaire, *q. v.*
renóir *for* reanóir, *q. v.*
rentuinn *for* reanouine, *q. v. and* ouine.
reov, *n. m., gen.* reoiv, *pl. id., and* reova, a jewel, a precious stone, anything valuable; *see* rean : connbolg reov, round bag of valuables; *par.* 5, *q. v. and note a.*
reoiv, *pl. of* reov, jewels; *see* reov.
rercinn *for* reircinn, *q. v.*
rét *for* reov, *q. v.*
rgéit, *also written* rcéit, *q. v.*
rgeula, *also written* rceula, *q. v.*
ri, *pers. pron.*, she, it; *acc.* í.
ria, *adj., irr. comp. of* fava, longer.
riav, *pers. pron.* they; riav-ran, *emph.*
rib *for* rít, *or* riot, peace.
rive *for* ri, re, rean *or* ran, *suffix.*
figine, *obs. n.* signs (?); *see note p.* 69.
rim *for* re, *pron. and* ran, *suffix.*
rin, *dem. pron. indec.* that, those; ó fin, from that; iar rin, after that; ann rin, then, there, &c.
rine *for* ríne, *q. v. and* rín.

ṙın,   ) *n. f.*, *gen.* ṙıne. the weather, a season, &c. ; áılle
ṙıon,  }   ṙıne, the brilliance, **or** beauty of the weather;
       )   ṙoınıon, fair weather ; ʋoınıon, bad weather.
ṙíne, *gen. of* ṙın, *q. v.*
Sıonnᴀ, *p. n.*, *Sionna*, the Shannon ; *see* ḃᴀnḃ Sıonnᴀ.
ṙıoṗ, *adj.*, lasting; ʒo ṙıoṗ, always.
ṙıoṙ, *adv.*, down, below; *see note p.* 54.
ṙıoċ,} *n. f., gen.* ṙıoċᴀ, *and* ṙíċe, peace, agreement, an
ṙíċ, }    atonement; ʋo ṗınneᴀʋᴀṗ ṙıoċ, they made peace.
ṙleᴀʒ, *n. f., gen.* ṙleıʒe, *dat.* ṙleıʒ, *pl.* ṙleᴀʒᴀ, a spear, a
       lance; ḃá ḟleıʒ, two spears; ḃá *governs dat. of fem.*
       *nouns*; ʋeuṅ ṙleᴀʒᴀ, make spears; ʋ'ᴀ ḟleıʒ, of his
       spear.
ṙleᴀʒᴀ, *pl. of* ṙleᴀʒ, *q. v.*
ṙlebe *for* ṙléıbe, *q. v. and* ṙlıᴀḃ.
ṙleʒᴀ *for* ṙleᴀʒᴀ, *pl., q. v. and* ṙleᴀʒ.
ṙléıbe, *gen. of* ṙlıᴀḃ, a mountain, *q. v.*
ṙleıbı *for* ṙléıbe, *q. v. and* ṙlıᴀḃ.
ṙleıʒ *for* ṙleıʒ, *dat., q. v. and* ṙleᴀʒ.
ṙleıʒ, *dat. of* ṙleᴀʒ, a spear, *q. v.*
ṙlıᴀḃ, *n. m., gen.* ṙléıbe, *pl.* ṙléıbċe, a mountain; *compare*
       ċeᴀċ, *gen.* ċıʒe, máʒ, *gen.* muıʒe, &c., **Slıᴀḃ**
       **blᴀṁᴀ**, *see* **note** *b. par.* 14; ṙlıᴀḃ luᴀċṗᴀ, *note b.*
       *par.* 33. &c. ; ṙlıᴀḃ ʒ-cṗoċ, *note b. par.* **20.**; ṙlıᴀḃ
       muıċe *or* nᴀ muıċe, *note b. par.* 42.
ṙlıʒe *for* ṙlıʒe, a way, *q. v.*
ṙlıʒe, ) *n. f., gen.* ṙlıʒe, *pl.* ṙlıʒċe, a way, a passage; ᴀıṗ
ṙlıʒ, }    ᴀ ḟlıʒe, on his way.
ṙlıoċċ, *n. m., gen.* ṙleᴀċċᴀ (1), offspring, posterity, race;
       (2), an extract, *see note p.* 54.
ṙloʒ *for* ṙluᴀʒ, *q. v. and* cᴀċ-ḟluᴀʒ.
ṙloınʋ *for* ṙloınṅ, *q. v.*
ṙloınṅ, *v. ac., inf.* -neᴀḋ, surname, give a name to; nıoṗ
       ḟloınn ṙıᴀʋé, they did not name him.
ṙluᴀʒ, **n. m.**, *gen.* -ᴀıʒ, *pl.* -ᴀıʒċe, a host, a multitude, an
       army; cᴀċ-ḟluᴀʒ, a battle-host.
ṙṅáṁ, *v. ac., inf. and part. id.* swim ; ᴀʒ ṙṅáṁ, swimming.
ṙo, *dem. pron. indec.* this, these; *with nouns* ṙo *like* ṙın, *re-*
       *quires the article*; ṙıᴀʋ ṙo, these; ᴀnn ṙo, here, in this.
ṙom *for* ṙᴀn, *suffix.*
ṙṗṙé, *n. f.* a dowry a portion.
ṙṗuċh *for* ṙṗuċ, a stream, *q. v.*
ṙṗuċ, *n. m., gen.* ṙṗoċᴀ, *pl. id.* a stream ; ceᴀṗbᴀıʋ ṙṗuċ,
       they skim over the stream; *see* ceṗbuıʋ.
ṙuᴀn, *n. m., gen.* **-ᴀıṅ**, sleep, rest ; ᴀ ṙuᴀn, at rest.

ruanán, *n. m. dim.*, *gen.* -áin, slumber; *see* ruaime.
ruaill, *obs. n. m. pl.* swallows; *see note p.* 69.
rúo, *pron.* that, those; *adv.* there, yonder.
rúil, *n. f.*, *gen.* rúla, *and* rúile, *pl.* rúile, *gen. pl.* rúl, an
    eye; leac-rúil, one eye; *see* leac.
rum, *obs. for* ran, *emphatic suffix.*
runn, *obs. suffix. for* ran, ra, &c.
cá, *v. subs.*, *m. inf.* beic, am, art, is, are; *see* cáio.
cabainc, *v. n.*, giving, waging, fighting.
cabainc *for* cabainc, *q. v.*
cáio, *v. subs.* 3*rd. pers. pl.*, they are; *see* acáic *and* cá.
caioe, *obs. n.* secrecy, concealment; 1 caioe *i.e.* a b-polac.
cailcain, *obs. gen. n.* strength, *adj.* sturdy, strong; caleap
    (O'R.), obstinacy.
caim *for* caim (*with slender vowel*), dead, still, *q. v.*
caim-neull, *cpd. n. m.*, a death-trance; *see par.* 19 *and note*
    *c. par.* 14, *also* caim *and* cam.
cáinic *or* cainig, *v. irr.* (*past tense of* cigim), came.
cainic *for* cáinic, *q. v.*
caipir, *pr. pron.* over him; caipir-rean, *emph.*
caipir-rean, *pr. pron. emph.*, over him.
caipirim *for* caipir-rean, *q. v. and* caipir.
cáirngire, *n. m.* prophecy, promise, fate; a o-cáirngire,
    promised; cír cáirngire, land of promise.
cairngire, *obs. for* cáirngire, *q. v.*
Cairrig, *p. n. m. gen.*, *Tairsigh*; Ui Tairsigh; *see par.* 1.
Cairrig *for* Cairrig, *q. v.*
camnell *for* caim-neull, *q. v.*
cam, *adj.*, still, quiet, dead; *n.* rest, death.
can *or* an, *n. m.* time; an can rin, that time, then.
car, *prep.* over, beyond, across.
caro, *obs. n. and v.*, marry; *i.e.* pór; *see* O'Reilly, carr, he
    gave; caroao, giving; *see* O'D. Supp. *in voce.*
carla,   } *v. impers.*, it happened, came to pass, he came;
carluig, }    carla a mág iongancac é, it chanced him
    (to be) in a wonderful plain; *Faghail craoibhe.*
carlaic, *obs. v.* threw, cast, (O'R.); oo cuir re, *par.* 19.
ceac, *n. m.*, *gen.* cige, *dat.* cig, *pl.* cigce, a house; ann a
    cig, in his house.
ceacc, *v. n.*, coming, to come; *inf. of* cig.
Ceamair, *p. n. f.*, *gen.* Ceamrac, *dat.* -raig, *Teamhair*; *see*
    O'Don. Supp. *in voce*; Ceamair na riog, Tara of the
    kings; Ceamair luacra, *Teamhair Luachra*, *see note*
    *b. par.* 2 *and* 11.
Ceamrac, *gen. of* Ceamair, *q. v.*

ceann, *adj.* stiff, strong; ceann-ap̄naċ, *cpd. adj.* strong-ribbed; *see* ap̄naċ *and par.* 14.
ceann-ap̄naċ, *cpd. adj.* strong-ribbed; *see* ceann.
ceccaic, *obs. for* cizio, *q. v. and* cig.
cech *for* ceaċ, *q. v.*
cecoiṗzioṗim, *obs. v.* he plays; *see* impið.
ceið, *v. irr.* go; ceið, goes; *inf.* ðul.
Ceimle, *p. n. m. Teimle*, a man's name.
Ceinm-Laoga, *n. obs.*, a kind of charm; *see note par.* 54.
Ceinm-Laeza *for* ceinm-Laoga, *q. v.*
céic *or* céið *for* ceið, *q. v.*
ceiċeað, *v. n. m.*, flight; ap̄ ceiċeað, on *or* in flight.
Cemle, *p. n. m. for* Ceimle, *q. v.*
Cempach *for* Ceaṁpaċ; *q. v. and* Ceaṁaip̄.
Cemup̄ Luaicp̄e *for* Ceaṁaip̄ Luaċp̄a; *see* Ceaṁaip̄.
cenð *or* cenn, *for* ceann, *q. v.*
cep̄caip̄, *obs. v.*, cut; *i.e.* zeap̄p̄; *see* ceap̄zað, O'D. Supp.
céc *for* céic *or* céið; *see* ceið.
cecheð *for* ceiċeað, flight.
cí, *obs. n.*, design, intention; ap̄ cí, about to; ap̄ cí ðo ṁap̄bað, about to slay thee.
cic *for* cig, *q. v.* comes.
cicic *for* cizið, they come; *q. v. and* cig.
cicp̄ium, *obs. for* cig p̄e, he comes.
cicp̄um, *obs. for* cig, *and* p̄e *or* p̄an.
cig, *v. irr., inf.* ceaċc, comes; cig Liom, it comes with me, I can; ní cig Linn, we cannot. (*Idioms*.)
cig *for* cig; *see under* ceaċ.
cig, *dat. of* ceaċ, a house, *q. v.*
cizið, *v. irr.* 3rd. *pers. pl. pres.*, they come.
cimċioll, *n. m., gen.* -ċill; a circuit, a round; a ð-cimċioll, *cpd. prep.*, (*governing genitive*), about; 'na ċimċioll, concerning him.
cimnap̄, *obs. v. hist. pres. tense, i.e.* ceiLeaðnap̄. *q. v.* bids, takes, leaves; ciomnaim, I leave, I bequeath.
cimp̄aize, *v. obs.* gathers, presses; ciomp̄uizim, I collect; O'Reilly; *see* p̄áip̄zið.
cinnep̄naċ *for* ceannap̄naċ, *q. v.*
cóċap̄, *n. m., gen.* -aip̄, a causeway; coċap̄ zLonða, *see* zLonða, *and note on par.* 46.
coccbaið *for* cózaið, *q. v.*
cocuip̄, *obs. v.* came, was put; *par.* 19.
cózaið, *v. acc.* 3rd. *pers. pres.* lifts, raises.
coimLið, *obs. for* coimLið, eats; *see* comLap̄.
comaiLc, *v. n. m.*, eating; ð'a ċomaiLc, for its eating.

ċomlair, 2*nd. pers. sing. past, of* comail, eat, you ate ; ap ċomlair, didst thou eat?
ċomlar, 1*st. pers. past.* I did eat ; níor ċomlar, I ate not.
comlar, *hist. pres. tense*, eats ; *par.* 54.
comlir *for* ċomlar, *q. v.*
Torba, *p. n. f., Torba*, a woman's name.
torcuir, *v. obs.* (*see* pocair *and par.* 7 *and* 11), was slain ; torchair, fell, or was killed ; O'Don. Supp.
torraċ, *adj.*, fruitful, pregnant.
trá, *expletive* ; *see note a. par.* 4.
trá *for* tráċ, time, &c. ; *q. v.*
tráċt, *v. n. m.*, treating, talking of ; gan tráċt air, without touching on it ; *see* cro.
tracht *for* tráċt, *q. v.*
trarcraid *for* trargraid. *q. v.*
trargraid *or* treargraid, slew, slaughtered.
tráċ *n. m.* time, occasion ; an tráċ, when.
treid, *n. obs.* three things.
trén *for* treun, *q. v.*
Trenmóir *for* Treunmóir *gen. ; see* Treunmór.
treun, *adj., comp.* tréine, brave, strong, valiant, mighty ; go ró-ṫreun, very bravely.
Treunmóir, *gen. of* Treunmór, *q. v.*
Treunmór, *p. n. m. Treunmor*, or Treun the great, one of Fionn's ancestors.
tré *or* trí, *prep.* through.
trí, *num. adj. card.* three.
tria *for* tré, through.
triall *v. ac., inf. id.* go, proceed ; triall, went.
trian, *n. m.* a third part ; a d-trian, the third part of their number ; dá d-trian, two-thirds.
tríċe *or* tríci, *pr. pron.* through her.
trom, *adj., comp.* troime, heavy, pregnant.
tu, *pers. pron.* thou ; tura, *emph.*
ṫu, *pers. pron. acc. and second. form*, thee, thou.
tuaċ, *n. m.* a race, a people, a tribe, a country.
tuc *for* tug, *q. v. and* ror tuc.
tucad *for* tugaḋ, *pass. past, q. v.*
tucaḋh *for* tucaḋ *and* tugaḋ, *q. v.*
tucrat *obs. for* tug riad ; *see* tug.
tuctach, *obs. adj.* shapely.
tug, *v. irr. past tense of* beirim, bore, gave.
tug *for* ṫug, *q. v.*
tugaḋ, *past pass. of irr. v.* beirim, I give : was given, waged, fought ; tugaḋ an caṫ, the battle was fought.

tugaó *for* tugaú, *q. v.*
tugaíú *for* tugaú, *q. v. and* tug.
tuit, *v. ac., inf.* tuitim *or* tuiceam, falls; oo tuit, fell.
tuinn, *obs. n.*, *see* ren-tuinn *and* ouine.
tuigtim, *v. irr. obs.* cover; *see* tuigteap.
tuigteap, *v. irr.* cover, thatch.
Tulċa *p. n. m. Tulcha,* a man's name.
túp, *n. m., gen.* cúip, a beginning; aip o-túp, at first.
tupa, *pers. pron. emph.* thee; *see* tu.
ua, *n. m., gen. and pl.* uí, a grandson, a descendant; uí Tairpig, the *uí* Tairsigh; *see* uí *and* Tairpig.
uaóaib *for* uaó *or* uaíó, from him; *see* uaíó.
uaíóib *for* uaċa, from them, *or* uaíóib, from ye.
uaíó, *pron.* from him.
uainn, *pr. pron.* from us.
uaiṅbeoil, *obs. adj.*, *see* puap *and* puaip, *dat.*, cold.
uaitib *for* uaċa, from them, *or* uaíóib, *q. v.*
uaitib, *pr. pron.* from ye or you.
uaċa, *pr. pron.*, from them.
uaċbáp, *n. m., gen.* -áip, terror, dread.
uato *for* uaċa, *q. v.*
uċt, *n. m., gen.* uċta *or* oċta, *pl. id.*, the breast, the bosom; i n-a h-uċt, to her breast.
úo, *indec. pron.*, that yonder.
uí, *gen. and pl.* of ua, *q. v.*
uíle *or* uile, *indef. pron. indec.* all, the whole.
uim *or* um *or* íom, *prep.* about; concerning.
uime, *prep.* about; *pr. pron.* about him.
Uipgpeann, *p. n. m.*, *gen.* -inn, *Uirgreann*, a man's name.
um *or* uim, *prep.* about, concerning; um an, *prep. and art*, about the (*see* imon).
umoppo *or* iomoppo, *q. v. conj.* but, also, however; *also used as an expletive*; *adv.* moreover.
'ip, *intens. par.* very; *generally used with adjectives signifying bad* qualities, *as* upgpánoa, very ugly; *compare* pap.
upċup *for* upċup, *q. v.*
upċup, *n. m., gen.* -uip, a shot, a cast, a throw; upċup o'a ṗleig, a cast of his spear.
upgpanoa *for* up-gpánoa, *q. v.*
upgpánoa, *cpd. adj.* very ugly; *see* up.
Uipgpeno *for* Uipgpeann, *q. v.*
uppaige *for* uppuige, *q. v.*
uppuige, *v. n.*, prayer, seeking, watching, praying for; *see note a. par.* 51. ag uppuige, watching.

# LIST OF IRISH BOOKS

SELECTED FOR THE

*Intermediate Education Course*

BY THE

### Commissioners of Intermediate Education,

AND FOR THE IRISH PROGRAMME OF THE

### Commissioners of National Education.

*Sold by the Publishers to the Gaelic Union.*

---

## INTERMEDIATE.

### JUNIOR GRADE.

|  | £ | s. | d. |
|---|---|---|---|
| College Irish Grammar. By the Very Rev. Ulick J. Canon Bourke, P.P., M.R.I.A. New Edition (under the auspices of the Society for the Preservation of the Irish Language). Fcap. 8vo, cloth | 0 | 2 | 6 |
| School Irish Grammar. By P. W. Joyce, LL.D., T.C.D., M.R.I.A. Fcap. 8vo, cloth, | 0 | 1 | 0 |
| ——— Part I., in wrapper, | 0 | 0 | 6 |
| Laoidh Oisín air Thír na n-óg; or, The Lay of Oisín on the Land of the Young; for the use of schools, with new Translation, Notes, and Vocabulary, Gaelic Union publications. Fcap. 8vo, wrapper, 9d.; same in cloth, | 0 | 1 | 0 |
| Toruigheacht Dhiarmuda agus Ghrainne; or, the Pursuit of Diarmuid and Grainne ("Transactions of Ossianic Society," vol. 3.) The work *complete*, edited with Translation, Notes, &c., by Standish Hayes O'Grady. 8vo, cloth, *net*, | 0 | 3 | 6 |
| ——————— Part I. Published by the Society for the Preservation of the Irish Language. Wrapper, 8vo, 1s.; cloth, | 0 | 1 | 6 |

## MIDDLE GRADE.

| | £ | s. | d. |
|---|---|---|---|
| Grammars, as above. | | | |
| Foras Feasa air Eirinn; or, Dr. Keating's History of Ireland in the original Irish, with new Translation, Notes, and Vocabulary, for use of schools. Book I. Part I. Gaelic Union publications. Wrapper, 1s. 4d.; cloth, | 0 | 2 | 0 |
| Pursuit of Diarmuid and Grainne, as above (part 2, pp. 120-194) Ossianic Society, vol. 3, *net*, | 0 | 3 | 6 |
| Title and Introduction to Mac Firbis' Book of Genealogies (1879). In O'Curry's "Lectures on MS. Materials of Ancient Irish History." 1 vol., cloth, | 0 | 7 | 6 |
| Imtheacht na Tromdhaimhe; or, Proceedings of the Great Bardic Institution ("Transactions of Ossianic Society," vol. 5). (1880). The work *complete*, edited with Translation, Notes, etc., by Professor Connellan, 8vo, cloth, *net*, | 0 | 3 | 6 |

### SENIOR GRADE.

| | £ | s. | d. |
|---|---|---|---|
| Grammar of the Irish Language. By John O'Donovan, LL.D., M.R.I.A. 8vo, cloth, *net*, | 0 | 12 | 0 |
| Imtheacht na Tromdhaimhe, *complete*. (1880). See "Middle Grade," above, 1 vol. 8vo, cloth, *net*, | 0 | 3 | 6 |
| Mac-ghníomhartha Fhinn; or, the Youthful Exploits of Fionn, son of Cumhall. New edition, with new literal Translation, Notes, Vocabulary, map. etc., for the use of Schools. Gaelic Union publications, in wrapper, | 0 | 1 | 0 |
| ——— Same in Ossianic Society, vol. 4, *net*, | 0 | 3 | 6 |
| Faghail craoibhe Chormaic mic Airt; or, The Finding of the Fairy-branch by King Cormac, son of Art. New edition, with literal Translation, Notes, and Vocabulary, for use of schools. Gaelic Union publications. *Nearly ready.* | | | |
| ——— Same in Ossianic Society, vol. 3, *net*, | 0 | 3 | 6 |
| Comhrac Firdiad; or, the Fight of Ferdia: and Aonach Carmain; or, the Fair of Carman (1879). In O'Curry's "Lectures on the Manners and Customs of the Ancient Irish" (vol. 3, *Appendix;*) "Questions on Archæology," etc., *in same*, 3 vols, 8vo, cloth, | 2 | 2 | 0 |
| Celtic Literature. O'Curry's "Lectures on the M,S. Materials of Ancient Irish History," (including all required for Examination). 1 vol., 8vo, 776 pp., cloth, *net*, | 0 | 7 | 6 |

*The books marked 1879 and 1880 are not retained on the Programme for 1881.*

## FOR NATIONAL SCHOOLS' IRISH PROGRAMME.

| | | | |
|---|---|---|---|
| School Irish Grammar. By P. W. Joyce, LL. D., T.C.D., M.R.I.A. Fcap 8vo, cloth, | 0 | 1 | 0 |
| ——— Part I., in wrapper | 0 | 0 | 6 |
| First Irish Book. Published for the Society for the Preservation of the Irish Language. 18mo, wrapper, | 0 | 0 | 2 |
| Second Irish Book. Published for the Society for the Preservation of the Irish Language. 18mo., wrapper, | 0 | 0 | 4 |
| Irish Phrase-Book. Gaelic Union Publications, *in preparation*. | | | |
| Laoidh Oisín air Thír na n-Óg; or, the Lay of Oisin on the Land of the Young, new edition for the use of Schools, with new Literal Translations, Copious Vocabulary, and Useful Notes, Gaelic Union Publications. Fcap 8vo, pp. 128, wrapper, 9d.; cloth, | 0 | 1 | 0 |
| ——— Same in Ossianic Society, vol. 4, *net* | 0 | 3 | 6 |
| First Gaelic Book. In three parts. Published for the Gaelic Union. Lessons in Gaelic. Nos. 1, 2, 3. *Each* 1d., | 0 | 0 | 3 |
| Lessons in Gaelic. No. 4. Second Gaelic Book. Part I., | 0 | 0 | 1 |

## OTHER IRISH BOOKS SUITABLE FOR SCHOOLS AND STUDENTS, AND AS PRIZES, &c.

### SOCIETY FOR THE PRESERVATION OF THE IRISH LANGUAGE.

| | | | |
|---|---|---|---|
| First Irish Book. 18mo wrapper, pp. 48 | 0 | 0 | 2 |
| Second Irish Book. ,, ,. 112 | 0 | 0 | 4 |
| Third Irish Book. ,, ,, 150 | 0 | 0 | 6 |
| Irish Head-line Copy Book. 4to | 0 | 0 | 2 |
| Pursuit of Diarmuid and Grainne. Part I. With copious Vocabulary, &c. pp. 210. Fcap 8vo, wrapper, 1s.; cloth, | 0 | 1 | 6 |
| ——— Part II. *In Preparation*. | | | |

### THE OSSIANIC SOCIETY TRANSACTIONS.

Vol. 1. Cath Ghabhra; or, the Battle of Gabhra. Edited with Translation, Notes, etc., by Nicholas O'Kearney. *Out of print*.

The Ossianic Society Transactions—*continued*.

Vol. 2. Feis Tighe Chonain; or, the Feast of the House of Conan. Edited with Translation, &c., by Nicholas O'Kearney. *Out of print.*

Vol. 3. Toruigheacht Dhiarmuda agus Ghrainne; or, the Pursuit of Diarmuid and Grainne. Edited by Standish Hayes O'Grady. Fághail craoibhe Chormaic mic Áirt; or, How Cormac found the branch. Edited by John O'Donovan. Caoidh Oisín a n-diaigh na Féinne; or, the Lamentation of Oisin after the Fenians. All complete in one volume, with Introductions, valuable Dissertations, Notes, and English Translations. *Scarce.* Fcap. 8vo, cloth, *net,* - 0 3 6

Vol. 4. **Laoithe** Fiannuigheachta; or, the Fenian Poems, 1st series, containing Agallamh Oisin agus Phadraic; or, the Dialogue of Oisin and Patrick; the Battle of Cnoc-an-áir, the Chase of Loch Léin, etc. Edited by John O'Daly. Laoidh Oisín air Thir na n-óg; or, the Lay of Oisin on the Land of Youth. Edited by Brian O'Looney. Mac-gnímhartha Finn; or, the Boyish Exploits of Fionn. Edited by John O'Donovan: with other poems, all complete in one volume, with Introductions, Notes, and Translations. Fcap. 8vo, cloth, *net,* - - - 0 3 6

Vol. 5. Imtheacht **na** Tromdhaimhe; or, the Proceedings of **the Great** Bardic Institution; Elegies and Odes; Ancient Poems, attributed to Amergin, Fintan, and Dallan. Poems by St. Colnm-kill, Mac Liag, etc.; an Introductory Essay on the Bards of Ireland; Dissertation on the Poems of Oisin (or Ossian); on the Fiann of Eire, etc. All complete in one volume, with copious valuable Notes, and close English translation. Edited by Prof. Connellan. Fcap. 8vo, cloth, *net,* - - - - 0 3 6

Vol. 6. Laoithe Fiannuigheachta (2nd series), containing Seilg Sleibhe g-Cuillin, Sleibhe Fuaid, Gleanna an-Smóil, Sleibhe na m-ban, or, **the** Chase of Sliav Guillion, Sliav Fuad, Glenn-a-Smol, Sliav na Man, etc., edited by John O'Daly. All complete in one volume, with close English translations, Notes, etc. Fcap. 8vo, cloth, *net,* - - - 0 3 6

N.B.—Each of the foregoing volumes is complete and distinct in itself.

---

M. H. GILL & SON, 50 UPPER SACKVILLE-ST., DUBLIN.

# MISCELLANEOUS IRISH BOOKS.

|  | £ | s. | d. |
|---|---|---|---|
| Grammar of the Irish Language. By John O'Donovan. 8vo, cloth, | 0 | 12 | 0 |
| College Irish Grammar. By the Rev. Canon Bourke. 8vo, cloth, | 0 | 2 | 6 |
| Easy Lessons in Irish. By the Rev. Canon Bourke, 8vo, cloth, | 0 | 2 | 6 |
| ———— in Five Parts. Wrapper, each | 0 | 0 | 6 |
| School Irish Grammar. By P. W. Joyce. Fcap. 8vo, cloth, | 0 | 1 | 0 |
| ———— Part I. | 0 | 0 | 6 |
| Self-Instruction in Irish. By John O'Daly, Fcap. 8vo, new edition, wrapper, | 0 | 0 | 6 |
| Irish Grammar Rules. By Rev. John Nolan. 16mo, | 0 | 0 | 4 |
| Irish Primer, with Copious Reading Lessons (for College of St. Columba), 8vo, cloth, | 0 | 2 | 6 |
| Imitation of Christ. Irish translation, *illustrated*. By the late Rev. Daniel O'Sullivan, P.P. (complete in 8 parts), 4 parts issued, 8vo, each | 0 | 0 | 2 |
| Sermons in Irish-Gaelic. By the Right Rev. James O'Gallagher, Bishop of Raphoe. Edited with Memoir, copious Vocabulary, and English translation on opposite pages, by Rev. Canon Ulick Bourke. 8vo, cloth, | 0 | 7 | 6 |
| Reliques of Irish Jacobite Poetry, with Metrical English translations by the late Edward Walsh, Second Edition, fcap 8vo, wrapper, | 0 | 1 | 0 |
| The Pious Miscellany, and other Poems. By Tadhg Gaolach, or Timothy O'Sullivan. In Irish. 18mo, cloth, 1s., wrapper, | 0 | 0 | 6 |
| Scela na Esergi; a Treatise on the Resurrection, from Leabhar na h-Uidhre. With Literal translation by J. O'Beirne Crowe. 8vo, wrapper, | 0 | 2 | 0 |
| The Irish Language Miscellany. A selection of Poems in Irish-Gaelic. By the Munster Bards of the Last Century, edited by John O'Daly. 8vo, wrapper, | 0 | 1 | 0 |
| The Midnight Court: Cúirt an mheàdhoinoidhche, a Heroic-Comic Poem in Irish-Gaelic. By Brian Mac Giolla Meidhre (Bryan Merriman). Fcap 8vo, wrapper | 0 | 2 | 0 |

M. H. GILL & SON, 50 UPPER SACKVILLE-ST., DUBLIN.

# PATRICK TRAYNOR,
## 29 ESSEX-QUAY, DUBLIN,

Keeps in stock the following, with other valuable Irish works, well suited for reading books in Irish classes, for students of Intermediate and National Schools, and as prizes.

*Full catalogues sent on application.*

|  | £ | s. | d. |
|---|---|---|---|
| Imtheacht na Tromdhaimhe (vol. 5, Ossianic Society), on the Programme of the Commissioners of Intermediate Education, 1880. "The Proceedings of the Great Bardic Institution," which describes their tour through Erin. It is taken from a vellum manuscript of the fourteenth century (the Book of Mac Carthy Riabhach). The power of the bards—their use and abuse thereof—are vividly portrayed in this severe satire on their order, the attributes of the chief bard and his school enumerated, and his lays of praise and satire recorded. The "Tainquest," or search for the great poem of the "Tain bo Chuailgne," is here told, to which work—the *Iliad* of Irish literature—the present is an introduction. This volume also contains many poems by ancient writers, and is edited by Professor Connellan. In one volume, *complete*. Fcap, 8vo, cloth, *net*, | 0 | 3 | 6 |
| Laoithe Fiannuigheachta, or the Fenian Poems; containing the original of Miss Brooke's Poem of the Chase of Sliav Guillion, the Chase of Sliav Fuad, and many other poems by Oisin and other ancient bards of Ireland. Edited by John O'Daly. All complete in one volume, with close English translations, notes, &c., fcap, 8vo, cloth, *net*, | 0 | 3 | 6 |
| Manuscript Materials of Ancient Irish History, Lectures on the, by the late Professor Eugene O'Curry. On the Programme of the Commissioners of Intermediate Education, and invaluable to the Students of Gaelic Literature. One vol., 8vo, cloth, 776 pp., illustrated with 26 plates (*fac similes*), published at 14s, *reduced to*, *net*, | 0 | 7 | 6 |
| Danta Iol-chumaisgthe, or Miscellaneous Poems and Songs (by Moore, Davis, Byron, Mahony, &c.) translated into Gaelic by the Rev. E. MacCoy. *Texts and translations on opposite pages*, a glossary at end of each poem, notes, &c. Printed in large, clear Irish type of the most approved style. 12mo, cloth, *reduced to* | 1 | 0 | 0 |

www.ingramcontent.com/pod-product-compliance
Lightning Source LLC
Chambersburg PA
CBHW020110170426
43199CB00009B/472